# Introduction to

## African American

## *Studies*

### A Critical Reader

Dr. Frederick Gooding, Jr.

# Kendall Hunt
publishing company

Cover image © Shutterstock. Inc.

www.kendallhunt.com
*Send all inquiries to*:
4050 Westmark Drive
Dubuque, IA 52004-1840

Copyright © 2016 by Dr. Frederick Gooding, Jr.

ISBN 978-1-5249-0223-0

# contents

# introduction

In this introductory section, typically an overview is provided the reader so as to best orient and inform the reader of what is yet to follow in the ensuing pages.

As time is of the essence, this introductory session will take a different tack as there is another threshold issue that must be addressed, namely the meaning of this manuscript's title. The title is often the reader's first "point of contact" with the manuscript and it takes upon an often overlooked, but vital function in encompassing in a mere few words what hundreds of pages and thousands of words deign to express in greater detail.

This manuscript's title, "Introduction to African American Studies: A Critical Reader," is composed of two parts: 1) Introduction to African American Studies and 2) A Critical Reader.

Firstly, in considering the phrasing "Introduction to African American Studies," perhaps a careful reading of these five words subtly suggests an unspoken tension that should not be taken for granted. Namely, that the author is to convey information to a reader that is presumptively unaware or not fully familiar with the topic of African American Studies. Unfortunately, for many American high school and beginning university and college students, this is often the case. Despite vociferous calls for strengthening nationwide curriculum standards (i.e., Common Core) and emphasizing the internalization of more substantive facts through vehicles such as Advanced Placement (AP) history courses, one underlying concern is whether students en masse are still experiencing early exposure to the "African American experience." This is not to assert that our students are bereft of any exposure to

African Americans, but rather the question that remains to be answered clearly and convincingly is the extent of such exposure outside the pedestrian, brief and routine mentions of Harriet Tubman, Rosa Parks and Dr. Martin Luther King primarily during the month of February.

We answer this question with a clear and lucid argument gently woven within the text that African American history is in fact American history.

And *vice versa*.

One would be hard pressed indeed to properly tell the story of the one without invoking the story of the other. Yet, gaps in fundamental understanding persist.

To be clear, a generalized, broad-brush, sweeping indictment of the American education system is not at play here. It goes without saying that so many instructors labor diligently to expand the world view of students about all facets of America's varied past, while not shying away from the "darker chapters" in American history.

To this end, virtually any red-blooded American worth their salt should be able to readily and easily identify national icons such as Harriet Tubman, Rosa Parks and Dr. Martin Luther King, Jr. Many know that once upon a time a "peculiar institution" entitled slavery existed—and more importantly that this "necessary evil" thankfully ended many years before they were born. And of course, what breathing American alive today does not acknowledge and recognize the symbolic and political significance of our forty-fourth President of the United States of America being none other than Barack Obama—an individual who by all intents and purposes personally acknowledges a connection to the African American experience within his own family history?

Yet, the question remains, is there more to explore? Furthermore, if more people knew more about this history, would we as a nation be more likely to resolve current racial dilemmas that stubbornly persist?

Hence, the "Introduction." This manuscript endeavors to introduce or invoke new concepts and ideas surrounding the African American experience more so than introduce additional names and dates with which the reader may not be readily familiar. The text presumes that many readers have already been introduced or exposed to African Americans in some form or fashion. Yet, so many among us have received an often limiting, two-dimensional picture of African American history and have not been shown more creative ways to appreciate the full depth and breadth of a truly death-defying, heart-pounding and amazing experience.

After all, with a majority white population inside the United States of America in 2016 with African Americans only constituting 13%, there still exists numerous swaths of everyday communities with little to no sustained African American presence nor influence. This fact prompts the question of how often is the average American exposed to an African American from a practical, pragmatic and personal standpoint? If and when such contact is made, do many Americans routinely experience African Americans through their established power and authority up close? Or is such contact typically premised primarily for purposes of sports and entertainment from a distance?

A few moments of reflection will confirm for the reader that so many images of African Americans within mainstream media are skewed in scope towards sports and entertainment solely, thus many are simply unfamiliar with a larger array of ideas associated with the broader experience.

Secondly, the phrasing "A Critical Reader" speaks to the importance of not just experiencing new ideas, but also understanding them fully by wrestling with the attendant concepts and engaging them fully. Standardized narratives of African Americans must be questioned in order for forward progress to be realized. While the subject of history concerns itself with the study of "change over time," despite several landmark changes, there nonetheless have been numerous racial dynamics that have remained consistent about the African American experience over time. What are the nature of these seemingly intractable themes? We will interrogate these concepts within this text.

One such theme seemingly indelibly linked to the African American experience is "the struggle." Historians such as Jacqueline Dowd Hall make reference in their research to the "long civil rights movement," or the continuous struggle for recognition of humanity within an institutional structure that failed to acknowledge full citizenship and all rights appertaining thereunto—at least initially. Many intrinsically know that the African American experience is defined in part by disparity, unfair treatment or shall we say, *inconsistency* in how the world-renown theories of the United States' democratic republic were applied to those Americans hailing from the African diaspora. A simple visit to the local library will reveal how literally, thousands of books have been written about race relations involving African Americans. Moreover, many continuously debate the extent that such inconsistency still influences current social relations. Yet, before we address the present, it is helpful to revisit the past. Thus, in invoking the terminology "the struggle," we also are reminded that African Americans were active agents in their own history. More specifically, that African Americans struggled against something. But struggle against what exactly? These initial dark chapters of history must be analyzed for both change and consistency, or continuity over time indeed.

One of the concepts that will receive attention by virtue of "A Critical Reader" will be the enduring relationship that African Americans historically held with institutionalized racism. Racism, or the distribution of resources according to a hierarchy of race, was unfortunately woven into the fabric of American society from its inception, at least in relation to African Americans. If slavery constituted the first point of contact that many blacks had within the United States of America, and if slavery qualifies at the minimum as "unfair treatment" based upon race, and if slavery was normalized by virtue of the fact that it was also legalized, then this initial, dark chapter within American history must be recognized as institutionalized.

Presently, our task is to execute an "Introduction to African American History," a history in which African Americans were first introduced to the struggle for "life, liberty and the pursuit of happiness" through the potentially contradictory lens of enslavement. When using the term "institutionalized racism," it is important to note that the system of enslavement was not limited to a small band of rogue and racist rebels but rather, it was part and parcel of legalized American commerce for more than two centuries.

Many a U.S. President, or chief executive officer of a country founded upon the idea of freedom, owned slaves. The institution of enslavement, or "unfair treatment," by definition resulted in the restricted distribution of resources according to a hierarchy of race. If one was deemed to be African American earlier in this nation's history, the ability to acquire and own property, earn a living and travel freely were all consequently deemed more difficult to do. Now is as good a time as any to engage these historical facts from the past in order to best understand where we stand within the present.

# EXPLANATION OF STRUCTURE

Three primary ideas frame and shape the dissemination of information delivered for each module. Each idea is fleshed out through the following three components:

- 5 critical concepts
- 3 critical quests
- 2 critical questions

Critical Concepts are not necessarily comprehensive, but instructive of the idea presented. Many of the chapters cover extensive periods of time and a mere five data points may not do the entire era justice. Yet, this pressure is removed since the five data points—whether they be the names of individuals, movements, or places—all embody aspects of the larger idea. Then with the Critical Quests, readers are encouraged to explore the chapter ideas in more detail, with the five data points merely serving as a guide for an independent investigation of the truth. Finally, each idea is reframed through two Critical Questions for readers to answer. Many questions appear simple in format, but are designed to have readers wrestle with the larger implications of the ideas presented. These three components will engage the reader, requiring the reader to become much more active in absorption of the content. African American history is still alive today and cannot be reduced to mere facts and dates.

Thus, provided each chapter contains three ideas with five Critical Concepts, three Critical Quests, and two Critical Questions apiece, each chapter will contain a total of fifteen Critical Concepts, nine Critical Quests, and six Critical Questions for a total of "30 Degrees of Exploration." As there are a total of twelve modules of thirty degrees each, the manuscript provides a total of 360 degrees for a well-rounded introduction to African American history! This book does not profess to be an exceedingly exhaustive encyclopedia or a tenaciously technical textbook; instead, it is a critical reader providing an introduction to important concepts and ideas that shape and frame the African American experience.

To wit, **Key Concepts** regarding the African American experience that will undergo consistent development within this text are: 1) change vs continuity over time, 2) quantity vs quality of change, and 3) duality vs duplicity of systemic inconsistency.

Perhaps every text stakes its claim as being different from the rest for some good reason, and here is ours: after completing this manuscript, the reader will walk away having had a conversation with themselves about their own relationship with

African Americans. Again, by emphasizing critical thinking of concepts and ideas above names and dates, readers will by design engage in what we affectionately entitle the "Independent Investigation of the Truth." The reader must think for themselves about what the historical data is and what it means. Conversely, rote memorization will do the reader little good not unless they plan to audition for a future quiz show. For the reader who at some point must put down the book and engage with other humans, retaining a new, critical appreciation for seemingly familiar concepts may serve more useful.

Once new information and ideas are acquired, the question is whether the reader will arrive at new insights? Will new data lead to new decisions? Will key critical concepts lead to new conclusions?

Provided so, this is where the magic of history lies; we can still discover the truth together...

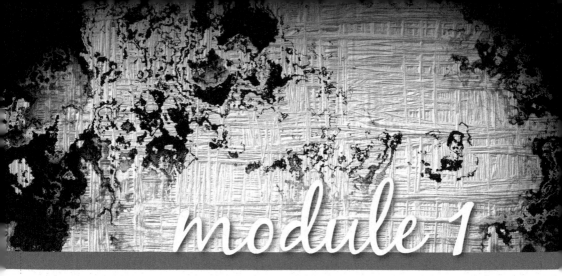

# module 1

# ENSLAVEMENT AND RACE

---

*"The story begins with the early arrival of Africans to America; it was a sad beginning to this evolving story..."*

---

## PRIMARY IDEAS TO BEAR IN MIND:

A. Most whites did not own slaves; but most whites shared a slave society.

B. American slavery was racialized slavery.

C. To "be black" was "to lack" during the antebellum period.

**A. Most whites did not own slaves; but most whites shared a slave society.**

## CRITICAL CONCEPTS

1) **Timbuktu**

   African American history did not necessarily begin with slavery. While 1619 does mark the first recorded arrival of twenty black slaves in Jamestown, Virginia, there was a history of these black Africans before they became African Americans. In other words, older African civilizations such as Timbuktu are overlooked and scarcely mentioned in most American high school history curriculums. Ancient African civilizations such as Egypt and the political value of its contributions to Western civilization are still in contention as evidenced by political posturing over whether Egypt is a part of Africa or the Middle East, for possible questions are raised as to whether (white) Europe or (black) Africa can claim dominion over the Western civilization that Americans inherit today. Although well known, Timbuktu is not the only African civilization, but is a representative reminder that the people who were captured and brought to America had an existence and culture that predated European contact. You as the reader are invited to research others. Originally settled in the early twelfth century, it became a center of learning and culture in the "golden age" of the fourteenth and fifteenth centuries.

2) **Jamestown, VA**

   Virginia's first Africans arrived at Point Comfort, on the James River, late in August 1619. There, "20 and odd Negroes" from the English ship *White Lion* were sold in exchange for food and some were transported to Jamestown, where they were sold again, likely into slavery. Historians have long believed these Africans to have come to Virginia from the Caribbean, but Spanish records suggest they had been captured in the Portuguese colony of Angola, in West Central Africa. This date of 1619 is generally known as the starting period of American African slavery (which would later become African American slavery).

3) **Middle Passage**

   In the days of the African slave trade to the New World, the middle part of the slave's journey (i.e., the crossing of the Atlantic Ocean) was referred to as the Middle Passage. From roughly 1518 to 1850, millions of African men, women, and children made the twenty- to ninety-day voyage aboard grossly overcrowded sailing ships manned by crews mostly from Great Britain, the Netherlands, Portugal, and France. Slaver captains anchored chiefly off the Guinea Coast for a month to a year to trade for their cargoes of 150 to

600 persons, most of whom had been kidnapped and forced to endure the march to the coast under wretched conditions. While at anchor and after the departure from Africa, those aboard ship were exposed to almost continuous dangers, including raids at port by hostile tribes, epidemics, attack by pirates or enemy ships, and bad weather. Although these events affected the ships' crews as well as the enslaved, they were more devastating to the latter group, who had also to cope with physical, sexual, and psychological abuse at the hands of their captors. Scholars offered differing estimates of the total number of Africans involved with the Middle Passage, with noted historian Philip Curtain citing 4 million and rival scholar Joseph Inikori citing a number as high as 12 million. Curtain is white, Inikori is black; each has accused the other of using data to further personal, political purposes. Curtain as a white male may want to mute the ill effects of slavery; Inikori may want to accentuate the damage done.

4) **Slave Society**

Most whites did not own slaves (remarkably only 10% to 13%); however, what we must recall is that a slave society was in full effect.[1] Think about how not every American currently owns a car, although we clearly are all familiar with them, use them, see them often, and in many cases fantasize about upgrading to a luxury model complete with all the requisite accoutrements. Slaves (although people) were seen as no different; one did not necessarily need to own a slave in order to nonetheless subscribe to the notion that blacks and only blacks were "worthy" of enslavement based upon their perceived subhuman status.

5) **Gustavus Vassa**

*The Life of Gustavus Vassa*, by Olaudah Equiano, was the first-ever slave autobiography, using his slave name, written after he was freed and living in England. The process of a former slave recording a first-person account is crucial in interrupting a narrative of slavery largely controlled by whites, given the systemic illiteracy of the enslaved as teaching slaves how to read and write was illegal. Vassa's account is thus all the more remarkable that he was able to not only learn another foreign tongue under duress, but was able to demonstrate command with his extensive and detailed descriptions in his narrative. The autobiography covers all of Equiano's life—his boyhood in the Gold Coast, his capture and transportation to the West Indies, and his success in business—a success that enabled him to buy his freedom. The autobiography was a success. It helped open up the opposition to slavery, which began to gather force in the later eighteenth century.

# CRITICAL QUESTS

6) **Objective: *To understand how a democracy could endorse slavery.***
   How did the United States Constitution "allow" for slavery to happen? There are at least three references to slavery in the Constitution:
   - 3/5 clause [Art I, Sec. 2]
     Representatives and direct Taxes shall be apportioned among the several States which may be included within this Union, according to their respective Numbers, which shall be determined by adding to the whole Number of free Persons, including those bound to Service for a Term of Years, and excluding Indians not taxed, three fifths of all other Person.
   - Slave trade clause [Art I, Sec. 9]
     The Migration or Importation of such Persons as any of the States now existing shall think proper to admit, shall not be prohibited by the Congress prior to the Year one thousand eight hundred and eight, but a Tax or duty may be imposed on such Importation, not exceeding ten dollars for each Person.
   - Fugitive slave clause [Art IV, Sec. 2]
     No Person held to Service or Labour in one State, under the Laws thereof, escaping into another, shall, in Consequence

of any Law or Regulation therein, be discharged from such
Service or Labour, but shall be delivered up on Claim of the
Party to whom such Service or Labour may be due.

Research these clauses and see if you can find additional commentary as
to what the "Forefathers" felt their significance would mean.

7) **Objective:** *To understand how whites managed to maintain an oppressive system of slavery for so long?*

Control was upheld through a combination of STICK (whip and lash) and
CARROT (coercion was seen as a more humane way of maintaining control
while avoiding "brutal" punishments). Instruments of social control were:

1) **Public**—Public control was maintained through local and federal law
and as recognized by the Constitution; the end result of this "official"
instrument was often dehumanization—owners exercised complete
physical authority over the enslaved as recognized by law (judge, jury,
executioner).

2) **Public-private**—The most common public-private means of control
were Slave Patrols, or organized bands of armed men (usually related to
slave owners) who carried out private objectives through public means.

3) **Private**—Manipulation of the mind to produce cooperation through
coercion gave many white American slaveholders a romantic sense of
pride that slavery in North America was not "as bad" as it could be in
other parts of the world (e.g., Brazil or the Caribbean). Social control
was often achieved by doling out necessities as gifts, granting holidays
or "time off" (usually connected to gift-giving), reinforcing vertical
bonds by incentivizing loyalty to "the master," encouraging informal
economies (e.g., allowing slaves to grow own crops, engage in craft-
work), hiring out of individual workers for wages off the plantation,
making promises to reunite family members, and of course, offering
manumission or the possibility of emancipation at some later date.

8) **Objective:** *To find "Forefather" involvement with slavery*

Forefathers like Thomas Jefferson were very much cognizant of the concept
of slavery. Observe an earlier draft of the Declaration of Independence:

He has waged cruel war against human nature itself, violat-
ing its most sacred rights of life & liberty in the persons of a
distant people who never offended him, captivating & carrying them into slavery in another hemisphere, or to incur
miserable death in their transportation thither. This piratical
warfare, the opprobrium of infidel powers, is the warfare of
the CHRISTIAN king of Great Britain. Determined to keep

open a market where MEN should be bought & sold, he has prostituted his negative for suppressing every legislative attempt to prohibit or to restrain this execrable commerce: and that this assemblage of horrors might want no fact of distinguished die, he is now exciting those very people to rise in arms among us, and to purchase that liberty of which he has deprived them, & murdering the people upon whom he also obtruded them; thus paying off former crimes committed against the liberties of one people, with crimes which he urges them to commit against the lives of another...[2]

For further understanding of the complex mind of Thomas Jefferson, read: "The American Paradox: Jeffersonian Equality and Racial Science," Alexander O. Boulton, *American Quarterly*, Vol. 47, No. 3 (Sep., 1995), pp. 467-492. This reading powerfully illustrates that even the best minds of the time were obsessed with notions of race. Many students today casually write off racial differences but we see then (as now) that one's race had significant economic, political, and social consequences. Thus, determining who was black and by how much was instrumental in determining one's whole life trajectory.

Finally, not to isolate Thomas Jefferson, but at least twelve other U.S. presidents owned slaves at some point in their life. Can you find out who? And which held slaves while in office? What does this say about early American democracy?

## CRITICAL QUESTIONS

9) **First consider:** Why blacks and not any other group? Under principles of Manifest Destiny, why did early settlers not enslave Native Americans? Many early Americans settled upon blacks as the "preferred alternative" for three chief reasons: a) orientation—the chances were higher of a Native American slavery escapee staying escaped if they were from the area and were more familiar with the topography and geography of the land than an African transplanted from an entirely different continent would face; b) if a Native American slave were to escape, it would be easier to "blend in" with local tribes for safety (even if not from the tribe) as opposed to an African slave; and c) African slaves were viewed as "more durable," in part because Africans came from a similar region of the planet as early Euro-American settlers, which meant that they shared many of the same immunities, which resulted in a lower death toll than Native Americans who often fell ill and could not recover from such contact.

10) **Then contemplate:** Is the memory of slavery treated with dignity and respect?

In talking about institutional memory, let us start with a common denominator: September 11, 2001. For many readers, this event may be the closest national tragedy in time. The 2013 Boston Marathon bombing and the 1995 Oklahoma City bombings also rocked the nation. The 9/11 terrorist attacks took on a powerful national significance as it was a multifaceted attack from multiple hijacked commercial airplanes that crashed in New York, Pennsylvania, and Washington, D.C. Many readers remember where they were that day, their reaction and the reactions of those around them.

Yet, consider how a pivotal event that happened relatively recently within historical memory is still in danger of being forgotten, according to some (<*http://news.yahoo.com/changes-surround-9-11-anniversary-commemoration-053639051.html*>). This presents an evolving question that we must confront. Whether it be 9/11, the Holocaust, the Vietnam War, the Civil War, or the legacy of enslavement and Jim Crow, how do we presently remember the past in the future?

Research and consider the following contemporary news stories. To what degree do they reference any of the ideas or concepts covered in the discussion about enslavement thus far?

- Black student called a "fraction" by bullying white roommates: <*http://news.msn.com/us/student-files-dollar5-million-claim-against-california-university-over-racial-hazing*>

- Texas textbook called slaves "workers":
  <*https://www.washingtonpost.com/news/morning-mix/wp/2015/10/05/immigrant-workers-or-slaves-textbook-maker-backtracks-after-mothers-online-complaint/*>
- Harvard Law School crest has ties to slavery unbeknownst to many:
  <*https://www.washingtonpost.com/news/grade-point/wp/2016/03/15/the-harvard-law-shield-tied-to-slavery-is-already-disappearing-after-corporation-vote/*>
- A Danish software company created a version of "Slave Tetris" as part of an educational video game:
  <*http://www.latimes.com/entertainment/herocomplex/la-et-hc-played-slave-tetris-kids-20150904-htmlstory.html*>
- Comedian Artie Lange posted what he thought were humorous tweets involving slavery and a black female on-air personality, Cari Champion:
  <*http://www.complex.com/sports/2014/11/artie-lange-sent-disgusting-tweets-espn-first-take-host-cari-champion/*>

## B. American slavery was racialized slavery.

# CRITICAL CONCEPTS

11) **Indentured servitude**

A person who came to America and was placed under contract to work for another over a period of time, usually seven years, especially during the seventeenth to nineteenth centuries. Generally, indentured servants included redemptioners, victims of religious or political persecution, persons kidnapped for the purpose, convicts, and paupers. As you read this material, you must suspend your current thinking. Many readers resist the concepts because they come across as repulsive, and instinctively they wish to distance themselves from such thought. Take yourself out of it. It is historical truth (unfortunately) that black Americans were oppressed in this country purely because of the fact that they were black. Check out this link to see how, although white indentured servants realized that as poor whites, they had more in common with enslaved blacks, a temporary alliance between the two to attempt to overthrow the power structure failed and in order to maintain control, the powers that were decided to punish blacks more severely to retain allegiance by whites, no matter their class standing: <*http://www.understandingrace.org/history/gov/colonial_authority.html*>

*Introduction to African-American Studies*

12) **Bacon's Rebellion**

Indentured servants both black and white joined the frontier rebellion in 1676. It was the first rebellion in the American colonies in which discontented frontiersmen took part. Seeing them united in a cause with black slaves alarmed and disturbed the ruling class who decided to punish black slaves more harshly in order to create a psychological division between the two groups, although both were disenfranchised in relation to the ruling elite. Historians believe the rebellion hastened the hardening of racial lines associated with slavery, as a way for planters and the colony to control some of the poor.

13) **"Necessary evil"**

A term many whites used when referring to slavery, to justify its existence. Under the auspices of Manifest Destiny, slaveholders felt that they essentially had no other choice when setting up the country but to use slavery in order to maximize resources on the land. This term also reflects the psychological conflict whites had with themselves. By calling slavery an "evil," they acknowledged on some level that what they were doing was wrong. Of course, the early American settlers had a choice; they could have elected to put in the work themselves. But because of their view of African Americans as less than human, they justified the placement of blacks within plantation fields as a way to build wealth more quickly.[3]

14) **Manifest Destiny**

Strongly held belief by many Americans in the 1840s that the United States was destined to expand across the continent, by force, as used against Native Americans, if necessary.[4] From the country's inception, many early white Americans have had an obsession or preoccupation with race when "moving" Native Americans out of the way in the name of Manifest Destiny and utilizing the "necessary evil" of enslavement as the most efficient means of developing this "New World." The controversy over slavery further fueled expansionism, as the North and South each wanted the nation to admit new states that supported its section's economic, political, and slave policies. By the end of the nineteenth century, this belief was used to support expansion in the Caribbean and the Pacific. Without going into a long and painful historical lesson here, suffice to be said that early Americans' enslavement of African Americans and subsequent treatment of Native Americans while settling the "New World" under principles of Manifest Destiny made for some possible contradictions to these heralded democratic principles from the country's inception. Consider this musical track by British artist Jamiroquai, entitled "Manifest Destiny": <https://www.youtube.com/watch?v=LAAl5bsTsXQ>

15) **"Unholy Trinity of Race Relations"** What we now know to be morally reprehensible was both legal and commonplace. What we must interrogate is whether we should not judge early settlers too harshly as times have changed and the men and women of past eras were merely "products of their time," or whether condemnation is in order because they knew in their hearts that what they were doing was wrong back then too?

At any rate, while not all whites held people hostage as slaves, much of America was still a slave society (just like all citizens presently do not own cars, but much of our society and daily life is significantly affected by them). Further, this slave society could not have existed for more than two centuries unless many significant actors devised working rationales. These rationales worked together to maintain a system that would normally wilt under critical scrutiny. However, there are three irrefutable historical themes that operated as an "intellectual shorthand" and provided white members of the slave society with just enough rationale to combat the rational argument against slavery (as espoused in the Declaration of Independence).

## Romantic Racialism

Romantic racialism was an influential nineteenth-century theme that propagated the narrative that blacks were actually *superior* to whites, but only within limited, subjugated contexts. Thus, black slaves were lauded for their physical stature and skill, but only in relation to how their production increased profits for the plantation owner. Blacks were seen as physically gifted and were also admired for their ability to sing, dance, and praise the Lord despite their oppressed existence. A false sense of racial comity developed where many whites were convinced that they actually liked and appreciated blacks, but it was not a deep abiding love or respect. At an early stage, blacks were primarily valued for their performances only.

Romantic racialism also emerged at the same time, moving focus from seeming social and intellectual deficiencies of black people and emphasizing their lightheartedness and willingness to serve—qualities of natural Christians. Thus, in the 1860s the more conservative romantic racialists pushed again for colonization, arguing that these "natural Christians" could only flourish back in their native Africa. This idea, which posited that blacks were docile, childlike creatures whose attributes allowed them to attain a level of Christianity unavailable to "naturally aggressive" Caucasians, had great appeal among abolitionists in the North who believed slavery was wrong on religious grounds. Moreover, romantic racialism arose as a response to emerging ideas about perceived Anglo-Saxon superiority and the need for a homogeneous white nation.

Currently in contemporary society, the sports industry is one of the few industries where based upon rules of meritocracy, whites have been forced to acknowledge exceptional black performances, or "superiority."

## Femininity

Femininity focused on the enslaved black's relationship with his white captor. The height of fantasy was for whites to go to bed guilt free at night, knowing that the enslaved blacks who worked at their plantation did so because they somehow enjoyed it or wanted to. This fictive narrative stems from the general *anthropomorphization* of races to genders, and the white race was seen as a "masculine" race due to its ability to build and design whereas the black race was seen as "feminine," or more docile and better suited for servile positions—whether male or female.[6] Hence, this narrative fooled many a white plantation owner into believing that the enslaved present simply had no other lot in life. For instance, Harriet Beecher Stowe's titular character, Uncle Tom, from *Uncle Tom's Cabin*, embodied this image of an older, nonthreatening, devoutly religious and fiercely devoted slave who would willingly sacrifice everything for his master. It is no coincidence a black character molded in femininity took firm hold inside the mainstream consciousness given the political climate of the time.

## Negrophobia

Negrophobia developed later in the enslavement era and was a preemptive narrative used to justify and defend whites against threatening blacks.[7] The only issue here is that such justifications often required great leaps of logic of which were ultimately immaterial to the user. Blacks were enslaved mostly by whites against their will. Many blacks resisted, rebelled, or at least thought about doing so. Many whites placed themselves in the shoes of the enslaved and thought about the anger and outrage they would feel if placed in such a position. Many whites then feared the "backlash" they might receive from the enslaved if freedom was ever obtained for all. Thus, any slight perception of black anger was to be immediately distrusted as dangerous and had to be quelled and subdued, and forcefully if need be.

Negrophobia later expanded to include the unexplained, fiery hate that many whites openly exhibited toward blacks. For instance, members of vigilante groups such as the Ku Klux Klan often "cited" fears of miscegenation, rape, and joblessness for whites if blacks were allowed to run amok unchecked, thereby requiring the need to keep the "negro in his place." This negrophobia fueled many of our country's lynchings and other terrorist acts of violence against members of the black community and their allies. Yet, very seldom have sustained, systemic mass attacks of whites against blacks been historically documented as a "justified" defense in response to sustained, systemic mass attacks of blacks upon whites. In most cases, the impetus behind tensions underlying this racial rivalry were sparked by Team White playing on the offensive side of the ball. NOTE: the exceptional cases of Nat Turner and Denmark Vesey's separate uprisings were neutralized and quashed in relatively short order.

While defeatist principles of the Unholy Trinity may apply to any and all persons, this country has an established history of employing them consistently and explicitly against blacks.

## CRITICAL QUESTS

16) **Objective:** *To understand the racial nature of slavery*

Notice the descriptions of the following enslaved persons; there is no mistaking that black became more than a mere "color," but rather a conceptual framework with which to categorize everything associated with the African American experience as inferior:

- *<http://hitchcock.itc.virginia.edu/SlaveTrade/collection/large/NW0305.JPG>*
- *<http://hitchcock.itc.virginia.edu/SlaveTrade/collection/large/NW0306.JPG>*
- *<http://aam.wcu.edu/projects/watras/slaveademily.jpg>*
- *<http://www.wisconsinhistory.org/whi/fullRecord.asp?id=3345>*

17) **Objective:** *To find modern references to the Unholy Trinity*

Romantic racialism—Have you seen any African American performers praised for their superiority, but within a limited context (e.g., sports or entertainment)?

Femininity—Have you seen any public mainstream images of African American males emasculated in contrast to white males?[8]

Negrophobia—Have you seen any depictions of African American males as being a threat to society or being "less than civilized"?

18) **Objective:** *To find early images of black slaves*
Search online to find early cartoons, photographs, posters, or other depictions of black slaves. What was the "black image within the white mind" and how has it changed over time?

## CRITICAL QUESTIONS

19) **First consider:** Slavery existed before early Americans employed the system; what were some key differences between, say, ancient Roman slavery and American slavery? Look up Roman slavery and compare how Roman slaves were identified, treated, and integrated into mainstream society in contrast to African American slaves.

20) **Then contemplate:** Explain how African Americans were viewed as being both the object of fear and fascination within the eyes of whites? For instance, blacks were viewed as subhuman and therefore bereft of skills necessary to integrate within mainstream society and thus were restricted as such. Blacks were not allowed simple courtesies such as the dignity of being able to eat at the same table as whites. This extreme segregation represents fear of contact. Yet, a fascination persisted. Whites still desired for black slaves to serve as wet nurses for their own children, apparently deeming milk coming from the body of a slave to be good enough for their precious offspring. How do you reconcile this possible contradiction?

### C. To "be black" was to lack during the antebellum period.

## CRITICAL CONCEPTS

21) **Dred Scott**
Scott had tried unsuccessfully to escape from slavery and later to buy his freedom. In 1846 he filed suit in the Missouri state courts for his freedom on the grounds that residence in a free territory had liberated him. Scott's suit finally came before the U.S. Supreme Court. On March 6, 1857, in *Dred Scott v. John Sanford,* after much debate the Supreme Court ruled against Scott 7 to 2, with Chief Justice Roger B. Taney giving the majority opinion. According to Taney, Scott could not sue Sanford because he was not a U.S. citizen. The justice argued that Scott was not a citizen because he was both a black man and a slave. Taney's remarks that black men "had no rights which the white man was bound to respect" came as a severe blow to abolitionists.

## 22) Margaret Garner

On January 28, 1856, Margaret Garner was facing recapture and return to slavery, when she killed her two-year-old daughter, and attempted to kill her other three children, in order to prevent them from being re-enslaved. Because Margaret Garner was subject to the terms of the Fugitive Slave Law of 1850 and was also liable for the murder by the state of Ohio, the trial became the longest fugitive slave case of this era, pitting a free state against the United States. The Garner case symbolizes Black women's determination to resist their enslavement. In a single act of defiance, Margaret destroyed the master's "property" and his progeny. The dynamics of slavery in which race, gender, and class play a significant role, help to explain Margaret's infanticide, her resistance to enslavement, and likely her resolve to escape from sexual exploitation and physical abuse. Toni Morrison largely adapted the Margaret Garner story into the Pulitzer-Prize-winning 1987 novel, *Beloved,* which was made into a movie in 1998.

© TheBlackRhino/Shutterstock.com

## 23) Frederick Douglass

Frederick Douglass was a former slave who became one of the great American antislavery leaders of the 1800s. Douglass was born into slavery in Maryland but in 1838, at age twenty, he escaped to freedom in New York. A few years later he went to work for abolitionist William Lloyd

Garrison, travelling and speaking on behalf of Garrison's paper *The Liberator*. Douglass published his memoir *Narrative of the Life of Frederick Douglass, an American Slave* in 1845. Eloquent, smart, and determined, Douglass gained fame as a speaker, began his own antislavery publications, and became a "conductor" on the Underground Railroad. In later years he became a personal friend of Abraham Lincoln and helped persuade Lincoln to issue the Emancipation Proclamation. He also was a strong supporter of women's rights. He is often described as the founder of the American civil rights movement.

24) **William Lloyd Garrison**

In the *Liberator,* white male Garrison took an uncompromising stand for immediate and complete abolition of slavery. Though its circulation was never over 3,000, the paper became famous for its startling and quotable language. Garrison relied wholly upon moral persuasion, believing in the use of neither force nor the ballot to gain his end. His language antagonized many, including his good friend and ally, Frederick Douglass.

25) **Harriet Beecher Stowe**

Not until the passage of the Fugitive Slave Act (1850) was Stowe moved to write upon the subject of enslavement. *Uncle Tom's Cabin,* first published serially (1851–52) in the abolitionist paper *National Era,* was not intended as abolitionist propaganda nor was it directed against the South, but slaveholders condemned the book as unfair, and it also crystallized the sentiments of the North. In one year more than 300,000 copies sold in the United States and over 1 million in Britain. In addition, its dramatization by G. L. Aiken had a long run. The book was translated into many foreign languages, and when Stowe visited Europe in 1853 she received the bestowal of numerous honors.

## CRITICAL QUESTS

26) **Objective:** *To find legal restrictions upon slaves*

Look online to see what slaves could and could not do before the start of the Civil War. Be clear to understand that America's slave society was not the product of a rebel group of rabble-rousers who simply wanted to be impolite to blacks; it was regimented, official, and real. Explore to find out.

27) **Objective:** *To find the reasoning employed in the Dred Scott case*

It is not enough to simply gloss over the past since it is no longer present; take the time to read the *legal* reasoning supplied by the highest court in the land. The Supreme Court applied case law to invalidate black citizenship. It used logic and reason. The question is whether it used racism? Explore to find out.

28) **Objective:** *To appreciate the genius of Frederick Douglass*

Look up Douglass's famous 1852 speech, "The Meaning of the 4th of July to the Negro." Douglass delivered his address to a mostly female crowd and was quite blunt by contemporary standards. Douglass starts off ingratiating his audience with compliments about the American democratic system before he employs sarcasm to highlight what he feels are several inconsistencies in American democracy in theory versus how it is actually practiced. This is an example of early black genius that may have been overlooked in your history textbooks to date. Explore to find out.

# CRITICAL QUESTIONS

29) **First consider:** What rights to "life, liberty and pursuit of happiness" did blacks have? The 2004 Hollywood movie *Bringing Down the House* features a scene late in the movie whereupon Mrs. Arness (Joan Plowright) belts out in song "Hmmm, Mama, is massa gonna sell us tomorrow? Yes? Yes?" While intended to be the subject of comic relief, this song reflects a horrific reality facing many slaves. Namely, that at any point in time, precious family bonds could be ruptured if the plantation's "master" needed to sell a slave to settle debts, or to settle personal scores (e.g., selling the husband of the woman he made into his concubine).

Additionally, the phrase "being sold down river," refers to the speaker of this phrase being handed a difficult scenario, or a "raw deal." This phrase traces back to the era of enslavement whereupon rebellious or particularly contentious slaves were sold down the Mississippi River to plantations in the Deep South, where working conditions were generally known to be more oppressive with swamp conditions, mosquitoes, and high humidity indexes in addition to potentate slave owners who felt distance and protection from federal regulators in Washington, D.C.

30) **Then contemplate:** How hard did slaves work?

*New York Times* journalist William Rhoden wrote the book *Forty Million Slaves.*[9] Consider this analogy and how there are still traces of resistance to this idea of power and control over black commodities: <*http://sports.yahoo.com/blogs/nfl-shutdown-corner/richard-sherman-doug-baldwin-mock-nfl-in-press-conference-225024393.html*>. Were slaves truly compensated for their labors? If not, what would be the right way to go about calculating this "loss"? Or "opportunity cost"? Are black athletes today compensated adequately in proportion to the revenue they generate, not just for their "owner," but for the larger leagues to whom they devote their labors?

## Footnotes:

[1] Mink, Gwendolyn; Alice O'Connor. Poverty in the United States: An Encyclopedia of History, Politics, and Policy, Volume 1. Santa Barbara, CA: ABC-CLIO, Inc., 2004.

[2] In Thomas Jefferson's "original rough draught" of the Declaration of Independence, he analogizes the relationship between Britain and its taxation policies of the American colonies as akin to slavery. "Declaring Independence: Drafting the Documents." *Library of Congress*. Web. 12 December 2015. *<https://www. loc.gov/exhibits/declara/ruffdrft.html>*. This passage was later replaced with a more ambiguous passage about the-then King George's attempt to incite "domestic insurrections among us," primarily through unfair taxation policies.

[3] "Historians have long been aware that many southerners proclaimed slavery a necessary evil before the 1820s." Tallant, Harold D. Evil Necessity: Slavery and Political Culture in Antebellum Kentucky. Lexington: University Press of Kentucky, 2003, p.4.

[4] Manifest Destiny is defined as "the right of America to 'conquer, colonize, and Christianize' the continent of North America." Buck, Christopher. Religious Myths and Visions of America: How Minority Faiths Redefined America's World Role. Westport, CT: Praeger Publishers, 2009, p. 8.

[5] See Chapter Four, "Uncle Tom and the Anglo-Saxons: Romantic Racialism in the North." Fredrickson, George. The Black Image in the White Mind: The Debate on Afro-American Character and Destiny, 1817-1914. New York: Harper & Row, 1971.

[6] Id., p. 114.

[7] Id., Chapter Nine, "Negro as Beast: Southern Negrophobia at the Turn of the Century."

[8] Before answering, consider how the United States of America has a long, documented and protracted history of Whites exacting power control over Black bodies. For a historical narrative on the intersectionality of black labor/public displays of power, see Howard Zinn. A People's History of the United States: 1492 - Present. New York: HarperCollins Publishers, 2003; James W. Loewen. Lies My Teacher Told Me: Everything Your American History Textbook Got Wrong. New York: Touchstone, 2007; Michelle Alexander. The New Jim Crow: Mass Incarceration in the Age of Colorblindness. New York: The New Press, 2012.

[9] William C. Rhoden. Forty Million Dollar Slaves: The Rise, Fall, and Redemption of the Black Athlete. New York: Three Rivers Press, 2006.

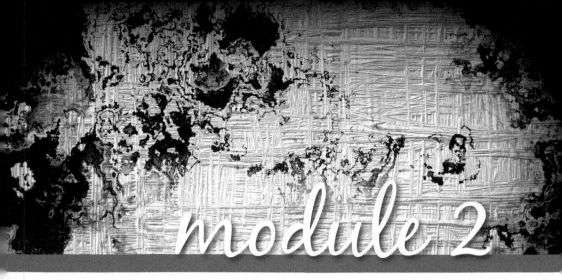

# CIVIL WAR

---

*"Pivotal period whereby physical freedom for all was secured; yet tensions leading up to USA's costliest war not fully resolved upon war's conclusion."*

---

## PRIMARY IDEAS TO BEAR IN MIND:

A.  The Civil War was fought for several reasons, yet tensions around slavery and race were a factor contributing to conflict.

B.  The Civil War was the most costly and deadliest war the United States has ever participated in for the entire history of the country.

C.  The Emancipation Proclamation did not end slavery; slavery was still legal in northern states such as Maryland and Delaware.

**A. The Civil War was fought for several reasons, yet tensions around slavery and race were a factor contributing to conflict.**

## CRITICAL CONCEPTS

**31) Louisiana Purchase**

In 1803, the U.S. government purchased over 800,000 square miles of land west of the Mississippi River from France in what would become the largest land acquisition in American history, also known as the Louisiana Purchase. Named "Louisiana" after the French "sun king," Louis XIV, the territory comprised most of the present-day western United States, including Arkansas. The Louisiana Purchase allowed the U.S. government to open up lands in the west for settlement, secured its borders against foreign threat, and gave the right to deposit goods duty-free at port cities (mainly New Orleans). In Arkansas, the Louisiana Purchase signaled an end to French and Spanish dominance as Americans filtered into the area. U.S. President Thomas Jefferson asked Congress to fund an expedition that would cross the Louisiana territory, regardless of who controlled it, and proceed on to the Pacific. This would become the Lewis and Clark Expedition

**32) Missouri Compromise**

An agreement in 1820 between proslavery and antislavery factions in the United States concerning the extension of slavery into new territories. Based upon the new and large acquisition of territory with the Louisiana Purchase, debate was fierce over how the new lands should be developed, namely through the model of independent enterprise practiced by hard-scrabble settlers, or the model of "entrepreneurship" which included individuals utilizing slave labor to develop their territory.

**33) King Cotton**

"King Cotton" refers to the agricultural dominance of the staple crop of cotton, which became a primary feature of the "triangle trade." Crops such as tobacco, cotton, and sugar were harvested in the lower south of the United States, mostly shipped abroad to western Europe, which then provided the incentive and means to insure and commission additional ships to venture from Europe to Western Africa to purchase additional slave labor that could eventually be transported back to the southeastern coast of the United States. This triangle trade would not have been possible without the ideal planting, soil, and weather conditions that allowed these products to proliferate more so than they did in Europe, thereby increasing their value and demand.

34) **Westward expansion**

While slavery also existed in the Northeast, the weather patterns and soil conditions did not lend themselves to "traditional plantation"–style slavery as commonly depicted within southern enclaves. The northeast employed more of a domestic, indentured servitude model whereas southern plantation models required large tracts of land and large numbers of slave workers in order to become profitable. These working conditions also influenced the political inclinations of whites with the northeast not as sympathetic to large-scale planation models, if anything, only because they personally did not reap any personal profit from these impractical models if employed up north. Many northerners thus saw slavery as an infringement upon fair competitive working conditions. Meanwhile, many southerners and those in favor of westward expansion saw slave labor as part of the American freedom to fulfill responsibilities of Manifest Destiny.

35) **Secession**

The process of state secession from the United States of America gradually started during the period 1860-61. In total, eleven southern states (Alabama, Arkansas, Florida, Georgia, Louisiana, Mississippi, North Carolina, South Carolina, Tennessee, Texas, and Virginia) expressed their dissatisfaction with the United States by withdrawing from the federal union, subsequently forming their own Confederate States of America, complete with a president (Jefferson Davis) and capitol (Montgomery, Alabama; Richmond, Virginia).

## CRITICAL QUESTS

36) **Objective: *To understand the tensions surrounding "states' rights" versus "federalism"***

Look up the Supreme Court case *Texas v. White* (1869) and see whether you agree with the reasoning that the U.S. Constitution does not allow for unilateral secession by states.

37) **Objective: *To understand the pressure the Triangle Trade placed upon the southern American economy***

Look up Triangle Trade and see what information you can find—is it readily discussed in high school textbooks? Or mostly reserved for "serious" academic journals? While slavery was not the sole reason why the Civil War was fought, an understanding of slavery's economic impact and its political significance for white male interpretations of freedom was an integral factor.

38) **Objective:** *To understand the significance of the Louisiana Purchase*
Did you know that the Arch in St. Louis, Missouri, was built to commemorate St. Louis being viewed as "the gateway to the west"? At the base of the Arch is the Lewis & Clark Museum, sponsored by U.S. National Parks. Look up as much as you can about the exhibits of this museum online: How much of this experience is romanticized with respect to the narrative of the "wild west" being tamed, mapped, chronicled, catalogued, and thereby brought under political control? What did this expansion mean for Native Americans already inhabiting the areas frequented by Lewis and Clark?

## CRITICAL QUESTIONS

39) **First consider:** Is it not without irony that the "freedom" to enslave others while pursuing one's own "life, liberty and pursuit of happiness" was a major factor of contention in contemplating the future development of the country? Explain.

40) **Then contemplate:** If you were to isolate the three most important factors leading to the Civil War, what would they be? What percentage would you allocate to race and slavery as being an instrumental factor?

## B. The Civil War was the most costly and deadliest war the United States has ever participated in for the entire history of the country.

## CRITICAL CONCEPTS

41) **Bull Run, July 16, 1861**
The Confederates obtained the upper-hand upon the Union soldiers during this skirmish and Lincoln quickly observed that the Civil War would not be a swift and easy battle. The Confederates got the best of the Union soldiers and Lincoln quickly observed that the Civil War would not be a quick and easy battle. Conscription was employed by both sides as a way to quickly increase the numbers of their respective armies.

42) **Antietam, September 16, 1862**
Known as the bloodiest single day in American military history where over 22,000 were either killed, wounded, or considered missing in action. This battle ended in a draw. Antietam and other bloody battles make clear that the war will break new ground for its brutality. Rising casualties prompt

Lincoln to threaten rebellious states with emancipation of their slaves. Both North and South begin to mobilize their entire societies in response.

43) **Draft Riots, July, 1863**

In New York City, unskilled Irish workers and other white northerners were convinced by leading Democrats that the war was a crusade to benefit blacks and revolted against the Draft Law, or first federal attempt at conscription, or forced registration for army purposes. This event showed how unpopular Lincoln and the Civil War were for those in the North and Midwest. Lincoln's waning support was then buttressed with the victory at Gettysburg.

44) **Gettysburg, July 1, 1863**

The Battle of Gettysburg produces the highest casualties of the war on both sides with over 51,000 lives either dead, wounded, or missing in action after three days of total battle action. Battles at Gettysburg (Pennsylvania) and Vicksburg (Mississippi) end any hope of southern victory as the North successfully repelled General Robert E. Lee's advances deep into northern territory. Further, it was when Lincoln dedicated a national cemetery in honor of the fallen later in the year that he gave the widely cited and well-known "Gettysburg Address."

45) **Sherman's March**

Major General William Tecumseh Sherman successfully captured the southern city of Atlanta, Georgia, and then sought to march out east toward the Atlantic Ocean to further compromise General Lee's army who would be between his advancing army on one side and those of General Grant on the other. However, Sherman is likely best known not just for capturing Atlanta, but for the way he captured the city, starting a new phase of southern deprivation not seen before 1864. Sherman was absolutely brutal in his tactics of using total destructive warfare to punish fallen Confederates, literally leading a scorched Earth campaign where everything was destroyed as punishment for rebelling against the Union. To show that such destruction was merely a psychological tactic to dissuade further fighting, Sherman was alternately quite magnanimous and generous with his terms of surrender. Sherman's psychological tactics have since been emulated in subsequent American wars.

The Civil War now becomes a bloody war of invasion and attrition. Sherman's army marches on Georgia and cuts the Confederacy in two; Atlanta burns to the ground (September 2, 1864). Yet, Lincoln's reelection ensures that the Union will fight the war until the Confederacy surrenders.

# CRITICAL QUESTS

46) **Objective:** *To find how impactful the Civil War has been*

Check out the link *<http://www.civilwar.org/education/history/faq/>* to see how many soldiers died in the Civil War as compared to other American skirmishes. You will find that more Americans died in the Civil War than in any other American battle and nearly matches the total of all other American wars combined. Why do you think so many Americans were involved in the Civil War? What do you think the impact was upon the population given the fact that the American populace was less numerous in the mid-nineteenth century than what it currently is?

47) **Objective:** *To understand the battle of Gettysburg*

In doing so, many a history or civics teacher will command middle or high school students to memorize President Abraham Lincoln's "Gettysburg Address" (e.g., "Fourscore and seven years ago, our Fathers brought forth upon this continent a new nation, conceived in liberty and dedicated to the proposition that all men are created equal..."). For a more contemporary take on the significance of Gettysburg, try viewing the Hollywood movie *Remember the Titans* (Disney) about an interracial football team that had to stop fighting each other before they could successfully battle other teams for championship supremacy. Within the movie, lead actor Denzel Washington gives a famous speech in Gettysburg. Observe, how did the movie makers incorporate the historical context of race and slavery into Washington's speech?

48) **Objective:** *To understand the repurposing of past political platforms*

For a more modern twist upon a modern take of a past event, check out the Hip Hop track, "Still Fighting" by the New York duo Smif & Wessun: *<https://www.youtube.com/watch?v=P016NQBnYiI>*. In this track they explicitly sample Denzel Washington's character's "Gettysburg Address" to his football team in *Remember the Titans*. How does their sample and use of the imagery of Gettysburg still connect to the real-life event of the Civil War? Why employ the title "Still Fighting"? Also notice how the Hip Hop track makes EXPLICIT reference to older, historical events such as the Middle Passage and the era of enslavement. What do such references tell us about the historical significance of such events upon members of modern society? What are the authors of the song track still fighting for?

# CRITICAL QUESTIONS

49) **First consider:** If you journey to the Deep South today as compared to developed parts of the far western or upper northeastern United States, one still might see traces of underdevelopment. Is it possible to link such underdevelopment in the South to losing in the Civil War?

50) **Then contemplate:** The Civil War is one of the most researched and "written about" topics. Have you actually counted or seen how many books have been composed about the Civil War? Why is the Civil War still such an important issue for current historians and members of the American population? What accounts for this continued fascination with this topic?

## C. The Emancipation Proclamation did not end slavery; slavery was still legal in northern states such as Maryland and Delaware.

# CRITICAL CONCEPTS

51) **Ambivalence**
The proper word to describe Lincoln's moral imperative to stop black suffering from slavery. The possible improvement of the black condition was a mere by-product of Lincoln's larger objectives of preserving the Union. "My paramount object in this struggle is to save the Union, and is not either to save or to destroy slavery. If I could save the Union without freeing any slave I would do it, and if I could save it by freeing all the slaves I would do it; and if I could save it by freeing some and leaving others alone I would also do that. What I do about slavery, and the colored race, I do because I believe it helps to save the Union; and what I forbear, I forbear because I do not believe it would help to save the Union. I have here stated my purpose according to my view of official duty; and I intend no modification of my oft-expressed personal wish that all men everywhere could be free."

Just a few years before the Civil War, Lincoln in 1858 stated: "I do not understand that because I do not want a negro woman for a slave I must necessarily have her for a wife" and "I am not, nor ever have been in favor of bringing about in any way the social and political equality of the white and black races...I will say in addition to this that there is a physical difference between the races which I believe will forever forbid the two races living together on terms of social and political equality."

Also in 1862 Lincoln favored a colonization plan that would remove blacks from the country as a possible means of eliminating the "race problem" afflicting the country.

52) **Emancipation Proclamation**

A presidential order in 1863 that proclaimed freedom to all slaves in the Confederate States of America. It was not a law passed by a Congress but a proclamation written by the president alone based on the war powers given by the Constitution. On January 1, 1863, Lincoln declared freedom of all slaves in the Confederate states, which had seceded from the United States of America. Its immediate impact was enormous—every day as the Union armies advanced, hundreds or thousands of slaves were liberated—until they were nearly all free in summer 1865. Not included were the Union slave states of Maryland, Delaware, Missouri, and Kentucky.

53) **Thirteenth Amendment**

The Thirteenth Amendment (1865) to the Constitution of the United States formally abolished slavery. Although the words *slavery* and *slave* are never mentioned in the Constitution, the Thirteenth Amendment abrogated those sections of the Constitution that had tacitly codified the "peculiar institution": Article I, Section 2, regarding apportionment of representation in the House of Representatives, which had been "determined by adding to the whole Number of free Persons, including those bound to Service for a Term of Years, and excluding Indians not taxed, three fifths of all other Persons provided for the appointment," with "all other persons" meaning slaves.

54) **Black soldiers**

The "struggle" was not over merely because many blacks joined the Union Army. Initially, blacks restricted from enlisting and slaveowning rights were still recognized. Black Union Army soldiers were always commanded by white officers and there was deep suspicion and mistrust over freely handing over armaments to black soldiers who might try to turn around and wage war with whites for other historical reasons. Yet, many black bodies were simply needed in the costly war effort. Once the 1863 Emancipation Proclamation took effect, even more blacks were recruited into the Union Army from southern states.

On page 497 of *Battle Cry of Freedom: The Civil War Era*, historian James McPherson notes that Union soldiers were just as cruel to blacks as Confederate soldiers; a Connecticut soldier wrote from Virginia how they took "two nigger wenches...turned them on their heads, & put tobacco, chips, sticks, lighted cigars & sand into their behinds."

*Introduction to African-American Studies*

White distrust of black soldiers was even greater in the South where slavery was still an issue. The Confederate Army did eventually allow black soldiers to serve, but were definitely late by northern standards. Black involvement with the Confederacy was not approved until March 13. On April 4, 1865, Richmond, the second capital of the Confederacy fell and General Robert E. Lee surrendered at Appomatox on April 9, 1865, less than a month after black involvement was recognized as a viable strategy.

55) **Assassination**

Lincoln was the first U.S. president to be assassinated while in office on April 15, 1865, *less than a week* after the formal conclusion of the Civil War. Lincoln was shot by John Wilkes Booth in the Ford's Theater in Washington, D.C. Booth's actions signaled that while the South lost the effort to secede from the Union, the battle over identity and heritage would rage on.

## CRITICAL QUESTS

56) **Objective:** *To learn of early "integration" efforts*

Research the 54th Massachusetts Regiment, one of the more well-known divisions of black soldiers fighting for Union causes. Can you find evidence or data reflecting how the black soldiers themselves felt about the enterprise? Or is their story primarily communicated through the recordings of their white superiors?

57) **Objective:** *To find the extent that blacks still fought internal discrimination from Union forces*

Research black soldiers' working conditions. Due to their black status, these soldiers were often still treated with second-class status—meaning, they had the most dangerous and dirtiest jobs, they reccived less and inferior quality rations, and had inferior equipment—all the while working to fight on the "same side." Find find further evidence of these disparities and answer why black soldiers would continue to suffer such mistreatment?

58) **Objective:** *To appreciate the continued tensions of the Civil War*

Look to see how many U.S. state territories still use or used the "stars and bars" of the Confederate flag as a public symbol. Why is the Confederate flag still such a contentious topic in current politics? What are the arguments that such a flag represents past southern heritage versus the idea that it embodies hate or support for slavery?

# CRITICAL QUESTIONS

59) **First consider:** Watch the movie *Glory*, starring Denzel Washington and Matthew Broderick. How would the movie be different if told from a black soldier's perspective rather than from the perspective of Broderick's white male character? How is our current understanding of the Civil War affected by the lack of inclusion of other black voices? Do such voices matter?

60) **Then contemplate:** Another mainstream movie, *Lincoln*, starring Daniel Day Lewis and directed by Steven Spielberg, was released in 2012 to critical acclaim. Some critics, however, observed that there was a lack of black voices in this movie as well—Frederick Douglass's brief appearance notwithstanding. Why do you think the tensions and debates over inclusion of black voices still continues today? What is the political and historical significance of such debates?

# BLACK RECONSTRUCTION

*"The country's first, earnest attempt to practice equality post-enslavement; revolutionary, controversial and short-lived."*

## PRIMARY IDEAS TO BEAR IN MIND:

A. Black reconstruction was the period immediately after the Civil War designed to help the country heal after a costly war.

B. Neither the Emancipation Proclamation nor the Thirteenth Amendment immediately ended the mental constructs that supported slavery.

C. Ironically, the Thirteenth Amendment created a "loophole" whereby the unsavory practices of black oppression merely continued, but by a different name.

**A. Black reconstruction was the period immediately after the Civil War designed to help the country heal after a costly war.**

## CRITICAL CONCEPTS

61) **Black reconstruction**

A period of unparalleled and unprecedented social reform immediately following the Civil War. Included in this package were social programs to help blacks, who by law were restricted from holding property and receiving education during the era of enslavement. Thus, the Freedman's Bureau created several schools, but the Radical Republicans from up North who thought this was a good idea faced steady opposition from southern politicians. Although initially propelled in a radical direction, this period lasted only twelve years (1865–1877) whereupon direct attempts were made to redress the inequities of slavery and its political, social, and economic legacy and to solve the problems arising from the readmission to the Union of the eleven states that had seceded at or before the outbreak of war. Factors undermining reconstruction radical potential include:

- Opposition to property redistribution
- Worries over reforms demanded by women and workers on the coattails of Reconstruction
- Deep and pervasive racism
- Southern violence and vigilantism
- Economic depression, 1873–1877

Reconstruction witnessed far-reaching changes in America's political life. At the national level, new laws and constitutional amendments permanently altered the federal system and the definition of American citizenship. In the South, a politically mobilized black community joined with white allies to bring the Republican Party to power, and with it a redefinition of the responsibilities of government. For the first time, blacks approached full citizenship by being elected into public political office and by serving on juries. Juries were integrated for the first time and there was the initial appointment of African Americans as police officers and constables.

62) **Dr. Carter G. Woodson**

Dr. Woodson was a black Ph.D. (while rare now, was unheard of in his time) who "rebelled" in an intellectual capacity to create a social and political space whereby African Americans would be respected for their constructive contributions. Gravely concerned with the existing narratives that assumed blacks had little to offer society, Woodson chose a week in February that contained both Frederick Douglass and President Abraham Lincoln's birthdays. We now know this manifestation of Black History Week as Black History Month.

63) **Thaddeus Stevens**

A white northern Congressman from Pennsylvania who insisted that the Southern states not be restored to the Union until they had been thoroughly reconstructed, arguing that by seceding they had lost all rights under the Constitution and were conquered provinces subject to congressional control. Stevens particularly wanted the economic and political power of the planters decreased and schools, land, and ballots provided for the freedmen. Stevens served on the crucial Joint Committee on Reconstruction in the postwar period, guiding much of its legislation, including the Fourteenth Amendment, guaranteeing civil rights for the freedmen, through the House. An adroit parliamentarian, Stevens intimidated opponents. Yet many of his more radical proposals were never passed. Many northerners were simply not ready to accept the social implications of radical measures designed to uplift the blacks. Stevens's views on Reconstruction clashed with President Andrew Johnson's more conservative course. The president's veto of the civil rights and Freedmen's Bureau bills in 1866 and his violent personal attack on Stevens prompted Stevens and other Republicans to break openly with Johnson and to push through a much more stringent congressional Reconstruction program over the president's opposition.

64) **"Forty acres and a mule"**

The phrase evokes the federal government's failure to redistribute plantation lands after the Civil War and the economic hardship that African Americans suffered as a result. As northern armies moved through the South at the end of the war, blacks began cultivating land abandoned by whites. Rumors developed that land would be seized from Confederates, and given or sold to freedmen. In January 1865, General William T. Sherman met with twenty African American leaders who told him that land ownership was the best way for blacks to secure and enjoy their newfound freedom. On January 16 that year, Sherman issued Special Field Order No. 15. The order reserved coastal land in Georgia and South Carolina for black settlement. Each family would receive forty acres. Later Sherman agreed to loan the settlers army mules. Six months after Sherman issued the order, 40,000 former slaves lived on 400,000 acres of this coastal land. In March Congress seemed to indicate plans for widespread land reform when it authorized the Freedmen's Bureau to divide confiscated land into small plots for sale to blacks and loyal southern whites. Less than a year after Sherman's order, President Andrew Johnson intervened, and ordered that the vast majority of confiscated land be returned to its former owners. This included most of land that the freedmen had settled. The federal government dispossessed tens of thousands of black landholders. The opposition to property redistribution: The business elements of the Republican Party fear a precedent-setting use of government power to expropriate and redistribute private property.

65) **Freedman's Bureau**

Established by Congress immediately following the end of the Civil War as a means to assist with the transition of over 4 million formerly enslaved individuals into "civil" society. Headed by Major General Oliver Howard, the Freedmen's Bureau was likely the progenitor of what we may now call welfare agencies today, or government-sponsored programs that pool public resources for individual improvement for the greater good. However, the Freedman's Bureau suffered from being a low priority and was inadequately funded and understaffed with personnel that was not fully trained. Despite such handicaps, the bureau facilitated medical assistance by building hospitals, and delivered rations to whites as well as blacks still suffering from the ravages of war. Likely, the Freedman's Bureau is best known for its contributions to education as more than 3,000 schools were built for black students. Many of the schools consisted of one-room schoolhouses that were vastly understaffed. Yet, these schools were deemed a significant improvement from the lack of a school entirely. Black students of all ages were directly impacted as most major black colleges and universities either received aid from or were founded by the bureau. For example, the historically black university, Howard University in Washington, D.C., is so named after General Howard. Congress, preoccupied with other national interests and responding to the continued hostility of white southerners, terminated the bureau in July 1872.

## CRITICAL QUESTS

66) **Objective:** *To understand how accomplished Dr. Woodson was as a thinker ahead of his time*

Look up how many black Ph.D.s exist in America today. Further, find out what percentage of Ph.D.s are black historians. One can only imagine how difficult it was for Dr. Woodson to obtain his education when he did. Moreover, what do you think about Carter G's philosophy of history? Do you agree it is necessary to dedicate a specialized time to think about black history specifically? What would he think of Black History Month today?

67) **Objective:** *To understand Dr. Woodson's visionary status*

To fully understand the forward thinking of Dr. Woodson, research how many other celebratory "months" there are in America. Understand that Woodson was the pioneer.

68) **Objective:** *To understand how promising Reconstruction appeared*

Search for a picture of the Mississippi State Senate in 1874, where you will see both blacks and women having unprecedented political access. Also look up the famous poster entitled, "From the Plantation to the Senate," with Frederick Douglass in the center. How different is this sentiment from the hit song by the rapper Drake, "Started from the Bottom, Now We Here?" Now finally, look up national senate and congressional representation. How much has changed over the years?

## CRITICAL QUESTIONS

69) **First consider:** Is twelve years of Reconstruction enough? Explain. Before answering, consider the cumulative effects of the following over the previous two centuries:
- Illiteracy
- Restriction from entrepreneurship
- Lack of political access/vote
- Disrupted family structure
- Impoverishment
- Lack of land ownership

70) **Then contemplate:** Randall Robinson, Ta-nehisi Coates, and David Horowitz have all written extensively about reparations, or financial compensation for blacks and their descendants for having endured enslavement. What are the arguments for and against reparations that you can think of? What would be the potential bottom-line cost of reparations if the government were to make some type of "payout" today?

## B. Neither the Emancipation Proclamation nor the Thirteenth Amendment immediately ended the mental constructs that supported slavery.

# CRITICAL CONCEPTS

71) **Juneteenth**
The purpose of Juneteenth is to commemorate the "late" communication of the 1863 signing of the Emancipation Proclamation, which freed all enslaved persons inside of Confederate states ("all states on the rebellion"), some of who did not find out until June 1865! As incredible as this sounds, we must recall that many who were enslaved were illiterate. Further, for many plantation owners, there was little incentive to "rush" to deliver the news. Many states in the southwestern United States observe this low-level holiday.

72) **Fourteenth Amendment**
Congressional approval of the Fourteenth Amendment (1866) applied penalties to states that deny black men voting rights and forfeiture of Confederate debts as a means to put the nation back on a path toward reconciliation and healing. The Fourteenth Amendment theoretically provided equal protection under the law, even though the Declaration of Independence already purported to lay out a political philosophy that did so, a philosophy upon which the U.S. Constitution was duly based. Yet, the amendment was viewed as necessary because in lacking access to property, and without a federal government or courts that were interested in protecting black rights from attack, it was almost inevitable that when an opportunity arose white southerners would disenfranchise and segregate blacks. The government was seen by many as more ineffectual and "corrupt" than the private sector and the idea of "laissez faire" thus gained ground at precisely the moment when industrialization began to accelerate. Black rights become precarious indeed.

73) **Supreme limitations**
The Supreme Court undermined black rights significantly in the wake of the Civil War. The Slaughterhouse cases (1873) ruled that states rather

than the federal government still exercised control over most citizens' rights. Further, *U.S. v. Cruiksank* (1876) gutted efforts by the federal government to protect black civil rights. This meant practically that many of the same tensions that existed between "states rights" and "federal control" before the Civil War continued and were vigorously contested. While the Freedman's Bureau was a federal initiative designed to ameliorate black suffering throughout the nation, in practice, the impact of such federal initiatives were severely limited in the southern states where the aforementioned Supreme Court cases allowed for states' rights to essentially trump what was viewed as federal intrusions into local politics.

## 74) Eight-hour workday

What is commonplace now was a foreign concept then. One who was enslaved simply worked at the pleasure of the plantation owner. Thus, in the aftermath of enslavement ending, one key question was what impact would the end of slavery have on free labor? Now that the playing field was made more level for all workers, more white laborers became concerned about the potential of them being exploited by larger capital interests. Hence, in 1863–1864, the number of unions grew from 79 to 270, with 32 unions organized on a national basis. Over 200,000 workers join unions during this span and agitation for an eight-hour workday began shortly thereafter, culminating with an Eight-Hour Day parade in New York City in 1872. The eight-hour workday was not legislated until 1938.

## 75) Fifteenth Amendment

The Fifteenth Amendment allowed for black males to vote; however, this breakthrough sorely agitated white female suffragists who felt they were overlooked. Soon after the Fifteenth Amendment's passage, the National Woman Suffrage Association (NAWSA) formed in 1869 under Susan B. Anthony and Elizabeth Cady Stanton. Its platform took the moderate argument by declaring that women, being inherently different from men, would re-

© Everett Historical/Shutterstock.com

store moral order and harmony if allowed the vote. NAWSA also upheld the racist ideologues of the day. Anthony openly declared "I will cut off this right arm of mine before I will ever work or demand the ballot for the Negro and not the woman."[1] In referencing black males, Stanton similarly opined: "No; I would not trust [them] with all my rights; degraded, oppressed [themselves], [they] would be more despotic with the governing power than even our Saxon rulers are."[2] Excluding black women from membership, it garnered significant support from southern women by asserting that the white woman's vote would maintain white supremacy in the South. In response, black women, such as Mary Church Terrell, formed their own organization to further suffrage in 1896, the National Association of Colored Women (NACW). Women's suffrage was not obtained until 1920.

## CRITICAL QUESTS

76) **Objective:** *To understand the slow transition of blacks into citizens*
Look up pictures of freed black families in 1870. What type of lifestyles were they living in contrast to their white counterparts?

77) **Objective:** *To understand the history of American education*
Look up Chapter 3 of Joel Spring's *The American School: A Global Context*[3] whereupon he posits that education was originally designed by the upper class with the upper class in mind. Look up early one-room schoolhouses used by blacks. Were these schools even designed to compete with traditional white schooling systems at the time? If not, then why were they built? If so, were they successful in competition?

78) **Objective:** *To find how difficult the transition was after slavery*
Opposition to significant change from southern whites and President Johnson was stoked by the fact that Johnson pardoned most ex-rebels. The return to power of the Democrats in the South leads to increasing deadlock between the parties in the electoral system that emerges between 1876 and 1896. Resurgence of Southern Democrats lead to near deadlock between the parties, from 1880–1896 with the presidency alternating back and forth in each election between Democrats and Republicans. The notion of an activist federal government is discredited in the eyes of many and the failure of Reconstruction sapped some of the energy from the women's rights and labor reform movements. As conservative ideals returned to the forefront, efforts to challenge the status quo became more difficult to advance. These political tensions crested during

*Introduction to African-American Studies*

the Hayes-Tilden Compromise wherein Hayes won the presidency in return for removal of last occupation forces from the South effectively ending Reconstruction in 1877. How might our political system be different today if Reconstruction lasted, say, fifty more years?

## CRITICAL QUESTIONS

79) **First consider:** The image of blacks depicted in the public mainstream eye began to change. Why do you think political cartoonist Thomas Nast rendered two different images of blacks? Look up his drawings during the Civil War in 1865 versus his drawings in 1874 during Reconstruction.

80) **Then contemplate:** This time period is also known as the time when blacks officially became "lazy." Look up through the Library of Congress online "Democratic anti-Freedmen's Bureau Campaign Propaganda" and study carefully the imaging and messaging. Do you think blacks would have been depicted this way if they were still under the power and control of whites? If whites had controlled the labor market for so long, why then, the need to disparage blacks as lazy? What possibly could whites fear of an underresourced, undereducated workforce?

## C. Ironically, the Thirteenth Amendment created a "loophole" whereby the unsavory practices of black oppression merely continued, but by a different name.

## CRITICAL CONCEPTS

81) **Ku Klux Klan**
In 1866, jilted Confederate soldiers started this organization. The KKK was known for having many high-ranking esteemed members of society as secretive, unknown members during the day, who would don white sheets and hoods as a masking agent to protect their true extremist political beliefs from being exposed. Membership peaked over 4 million in the 1920s. They were known for acts of vigilantism and terrorism; in addition to extrajudicial lynchings and church bombings, they were known for burning crosses on the lawns of black residents they wished to intimidate.

82) **Black Codes**
Immediately after the Civil War, southern states passed onerous laws to maintain their legal control and economic power over blacks after the era

of enslavement concluded.[4] The Black Codes were mostly enacted by former rebel states; an example of criminalizing black existence in the form of vagrancy in the Magnolia State includes:[5]

> Sec. 2....All freedmen, free negroes and mulattoes in this State, over the age of eighteen years, found on the second Monday in January, 1866, or thereafter, with no lawful employment or business, or found unlawfully assembling themselves together, either in the day or night time, and all white persons so assembling themselves with freedmen, free negroes or mulattoes, or usually associating with freedmen, free negroes or mulattoes, on terms of equality, or living in adultery or fornication with a freed woman, free negro or mulatto, shall be deemed vagrants, and on conviction thereof shall be fined in a sum not exceeding, in the case of a freedman, free negro or mulatto, fifty dollars, and a white man two hundred dollars, and imprisoned at the discretion of the court, the free negro not exceeding ten days, and the white man not exceeding six months....

83) **Convict lease system**

The Thirteenth Amendment of the U.S. Constitution, while effectively ending slavery, eventually authorized the use of freed slaves for involuntary servitude with the following clause: "Neither slavery nor involuntary servitude, except as a punishment for crime whereof the party shall have been duly convicted, shall exist within the United States or any place subject to their jurisdiction." Under the convict lease system implemented in the U.S. South after the Civil War, the state took advantage of this clause by leasing prison inmates to private companies that used them as forced laborers. This system of enforced labor ran from 1865 to 1920. Many southern states angry over a change in their "culture" responded by criminalizing the conduct of blacks (e.g., if they did not own property or have a job, they were vagrants who could be arrested, which was virtually everybody immediately after slavery ended). If you read the Thirteenth Amendment very carefully, you will see language that allowed for the convict leasing program, which essentially was an arrested black who was "lent" out by the jail to local plantations in need of labor.[6] NO ONE given a ten-year sentence or higher survived. For more information, see: <http://www.loc.gov/rr/program/bib/ourdocs/13thamendment.html>.

© Everett Historical/Shutterstock.com

84) **Sharecropping**

A land and labor arrangement whereby an individual or family receives a stipulated proportion of the crops produced on a particular plot of land in return for their labor on that same plot. The legal status of share-croppers varied over time and from state to state. Historically, many southern states classified sharecroppers as agricultural laborers, making them legally indistinguishable from wage hands, who worked on a daily, monthly, or annual basis on farms operated by others. Practically speaking, however, sharecroppers resembled both farm laborers and tenants in fundamental ways. Like the farm laborer, the sharecropper was allocated work stock, tools, and seed by the landlord, received wages rather than paid rent, and commonly labored under close supervision from the land-lord, who typically controlled most managerial decisions.

85) **Lynching**

This extra-legal means of exacting "justice" by the community was not authorized by the state or a court of law. Lynchings sprouted in number during this time period as Negrophobia was rampant and the narrative of savage, uncontrollable black men who wanted to ravage white wom-en's chastity and white men's jobs ran rampant.[7] Bryan Stevenson of the Equal Justice Initiative documents the embarrassingly high number of lynchings that took place. Activists such as Ida B. Wells spoke out against

the practice, and within northern cities, the National Association for the Advancement of Colored People would put out flags/signs downtown to inform the public "A black man was lynched yesterday" so as to connect the horrors of the South with the sophistication of the North.

## CRITICAL QUESTS

86) **Objective:** *To research chain gangs*
Watch the opening scene of the movie *O Brother, Where Art Thou*, to see a re-creation of how a chain gang operated. Further, look up featured singer James Carter's personal history. Was Carter properly compensated for his artistry? Or was Carter exploited ironically in a movie about escaping exploitation?

87) **Objective:** *To find out how sharecropping affected the south*
Look up the Barrow plantation and the dispersal of plantation housing from 1860–1881. In looking at land tract maps, it is evident that plantation owners still had vast amounts of land that required agricultural attention. If every worker was now free and independent, was it possible for plantation owners to even become profitable paying wages for work? Was the southern economy even designed for fair wages for fair work? If not, how then did plantation owners maintain power and control through sharecropping against an illiterate and under-resourced popula-

tion? Were blacks, too, economically oppressed in relation to working for whites, with the only difference being that now they technically "owned" the land they worked upon?

88) **Objective:** *To appreciate different African American barrier to success*
Emancipation and Reconstruction did not immediately usher in a period of black economic expansion as several factors limiting such were present: (1) The vast majority of millers, blacksmiths, carpenters, and other potential entrepreneurs were illiterate, according to the 1870 census; likely fewer than a third of all artisans were literate, skilled, but not schooled on the ability to maintain correspondence with customers, check accounts, and supervise payments to creditors; and were severely crippled. (2) Business of black artisans in slavery "had been to do work but not to get work," during Reconstruction; placing ads in local newspapers, hiring and firing employees, purchasing supplies, maintaining profit/loss records were difficult tasks for inexperienced blacks looking to compete, especially in view of "black code" regulations that charged higher licensing rates for blacks than whites (e.g., the State of South Carolina charged $100 license for blacks, $0 for whites), "no person of color shall pursue or practice the art, trade, or business of an artisan, mechanic or shopkeeper, or any other trade, employment or business...on his own account and for his own benefit until he shall have obtained a license which shall be good for one year only." (3) Obtaining credit from white banks, insurance from white agents, good deals from other small white merchants was a virtual impossibility. (4) Blacks faced social/legal exclusion from bonus business (e.g., restaurants, hotels, places of amusement). How then would these handicaps affect black descendants from such families struggling to compete generations later, as in present day?

## CRITICAL QUESTIONS

89) **First consider:** What do you think about the family-oriented, multinational company Disney making the movie *John Carter*, starring a former Confederate soldier? Does such a depiction trivialize the racial tensions typically associated with the Confederacy? Or was the movie a clever and savvy way to promote better race relations as Carter helps save and liberate a green alien race on Mars, even though he (in part) fought to maintain a life where fellow black humans would remain in chains?

90) **Then contemplate:** There are two statues of Abraham Lincoln entitled "Emancipation," one located in Boston, Massachusetts, the other in Wash-

ington, D.C. In looking up the images, in comparing the "body language" of the two figures, does the message "free but not equal" come to mind? If not, what other message do you derive and why?

© Everett Historical/Shutterstock.com

## Footnotes:

[1] *Wesleyan University.* "Black Women & The Suffrage Movement: 1848-1923." N.d <*http://www.wesleyan.edu/mlk/posters/suffrage.html*>.

[2] Brenda Wineapple. "'It is the nation's time': How women won the vote." *Salon.* 18 August, 2013. <*http://www.salon.com/2013/08/18/it_is_the_nations_ time_how_women_won_the_vote/*>.

[3] Joel Spring. *The American School: A Global Context; From the Puritans to the Obama Administration.* 2014. New York: McGraw Hill.

[4] With Black Codes cropping up in the aftermath of the Civil War, black life itself was literally criminalized. See "Black Codes and Pig Laws." *PBS*. Web. N.d. <*http://www.pbs.org/tpt/slavery-by-another-name/themes/black-codes/*>.

[5] James W. Loewen and Edward H. Sebesta, eds. *The Confederate and Neo-Confederate Reader: the Great Truth about the Lost Cause.* 2010: University Press of Mississippi, p. 238.

[6] See "Slavery by another Name." *PBS*. Web. N.d. < *http://www.pbs.org/tpt/ slavery-by-another-name/themes/convict-leasing/*>.

[7] Lynching in America: Confronting the Legacy of Racial Terror," Equal Justice Initiative. *Equal Justice Initiative*, 2015. Web. 12 December, 2015. < *http:// www.eji.org/files/EJI%20Lynching%20in%20America%20SUMMARY. pdf*>.so, see by Cynthia Skove Nevels, Lynching to Belong: Claiming Whiteness through Racial Violence. Centennial Series of the Association of Former Students, Texas A&M University, 2007. With case studies of lynchings fueled by early Irish and Italian immigrants, the premise offered is that the more racist outside immigration groups were, the more they proved their "Americanness" for mainstream inclusion.

# module 4

# JIM CROW'S REIGN

---

*"American society observed physical freedom in theory, but in practice such freedom was compromised by segregationist social policies."*

---

## PRIMARY IDEAS TO BEAR IN MIND:

A. We often think that once slavery was over, racism was over. In many ways, blacks had only begun to enter hell.

B. The era of segregation constituted much more than mere restrictions on water fountains and park benches as commonly depicted.

C. Leading thinkers were divided upon strategies to best combat the suppressive conditions of the time.

**A. We often think that once slavery was over, racism was over. In many ways, blacks had only begun to enter hell.**

## CRITICAL CONCEPTS

91) *Plessy v. Ferguson*

While many southern states instituted "black codes" which restricted black movement after the Civil War, racial segregation became a national policy in 1896 with the Supreme Court decision *Plessy v. Ferguson*. Here, the Supreme Court struck down a challenge to a Louisiana state law that called for racial segregation of train cars. In defending the state's right to legislate, the Supreme Court was not persuaded that the law was a violation of the Equal Protection Clause as spelled out in the Fourteenth Amendment. The Court rationalized that the Equal Protection Clause was not violated because the U.S. Constitution specifically spoke to political and not social equality. The court case's "separate but equal" doctrine became the latest legal fiction to justify discrimination between the races. The Black Codes instituted by the South immediately after the Civil War now became sanctioned by the Constitution and 1896 formally started the legally enforceable "Jim Crow Era" that would last up until the Supreme Court acted to desegregate schools with the 1954 *Brown v. Board* decision. The 1896 decision came only three years after the World's Fair in Chicago, which flourished with ideas of American Exceptionalism and perfection. In contrast to the black codes that affected mostly blacks in southern states, the *Plessy* decision established "separate but equal" as federal law of the land. Segregation, which had been on the rise before this, now descended completely across the South by law; and is confirmed in much of the North by custom. The *Plessy* decision was followed up by *Williams v. Mississippi* (1898), which limited existing federal power's ability to protect voting rights in the states, thereby leaving the door open to the use of literacy tests, poll taxes, and grandfather clauses in ways that nonetheless blocked black men's access to voting.

92) **Jim Crow segregation**

Segregation affected where one lived, how one created income, where one worked, and where and how one could socialize, let alone assert their power in public to change that which requires improvement. Jim Crow segregation constituted a collection of legal policies that observed and preserved strict separation between the races. Violators were punished. In other words, this policy era comprised much more than a small group

*Introduction to African-American Studies*

of ill-informed individuals who were just being "mean" to a couple of blacks. Whether whites conscientiously went out of their way to impose their social advantage upon blacks or not, whites nonetheless benefitted.

93) **Vigilantism**

Violence was rampant during this period of time as an extralegal means for whites to maintain power and control through terrorism and intimidation typically without fear of legal prosecution. While extralegal killings were the extreme form of this concept. It was not uncommon for blacks to experience harassment and confrontations, many of a physical nature, while simply handling routine errands or affairs.

94) **Minstrelsy**

Adding insult to injury, around the same time that blacks were restricted in their social, political, and economic movements, blacks also suffered from restriction of their image. During this time, publicly performed shows were commissioned and conducted whereby white actors would imitate and exaggerate what they thought to be black conduct all in the name of entertainment. Many audience members derived pleasure from romantic racialist notions that blacks still occupied a place in society that was beneath the white standard of normalcy. Minstrel shows were an example of unflattering and disparaging black image in the white mind, as the minstrel is entirely a product of white imagination. This image of incompetence was one that many blacks found difficult to overcome in their personal affairs.

## 95) Tulsa Riots

A lucid example of the violence propagated against blacks, especially blacks who were thriving economically, comes with the Tulsa Race Riots of 1921 in the Greenwood District of Tulsa, Oklahoma. Originally started by a rumor that a black elevator operator improperly propositioned a white female patron, whites went into the very successful and financially stable business district nicknamed "Black Wall Street," or at the time, the wealthiest black community in the entire United States and essentially burned it down. Many black businesses were destroyed, never to return again, along with several lives. In the process, no less than 191 black businesses and 1,256 black residences were destroyed, rendering a devastating effect upon a relatively self-sufficient section of the African American community not dependent upon white patronage for survival. A case for reparations/compensation has yet to materialize.

# CRITICAL QUESTS

## 96) Objective: *To understand the damage done to "Black Wall Street"*

Harvard Law professor Charles Ogletree took up the case of trying to obtain reparations for the surviving families who endured the horrors of the Tulsa Race Riots in 2003. It was dismissed. Look up the case and the rationales for why it was unable to get off the ground. Do you agree? If something should be done, what would be equitable? What does the aftermath say about the publicly shared valuation of black life? Did you discover the recommendations of the Tulsa Race Riot Commission delivered in 2001? Were all implemented effectively?

## 97) Objective: *To understand the encompassing effect of Jim Crow and its mark upon the southern American economy*

Do your own online research for images of "Jim Crow segregation" to see whether black and white facilities were truly separate but equal. In particular, attempt looking up school buildings. Think about the importance of having a high-quality space with which to learn and teach children about the world. How might having inferior educational facilities affect generations of blacks to come? Is data about black impoverishment today in any way related to such restrictions from the past? How does such past racial segregation and current economic underdevelopment compare to the economic and social status of Native Americans? In 1867, Reservations Policy confined Native Americans to reservations only to have the same reservations divided into individual plots in 1887 under the Dawes Act. Similar to sharecropping, the goal was to promote "free labor" land ownership and farming among Native Americans although four of five Native American landholders eventually lost their holdings after Dawes Act distributions, as a result of several bloody skirmishes continuing up until the late nineteenth century:

- Sand Creek Massacre, 1864
- Black Hills War, 1874-75
- Little Big Horn, 1876
- Assassination of Crazy Horse, 1877
- Wounded Knee Massacre, 1893

98) **Objective:** *To understand the significance of lynchings*

Observe how these murders were showcased and memorialized to share with others in the form of postcards: <*http://whosane.word-press.com/2008/03/02/historical-photos-and-postcards-of-lynch-ings-in-america////http://commons.wikimedia.org/wiki/File:Postcard_of_the_lynched_Jesse_Washington,_front_and_back.jpg*>

What do these photos say about our civilized, democratic republic? Fueling many lynchings were rabid thoughts of Negrophobia whereupon the narrative of the white woman as an ideal was exalted for her purity and puerility and was the object of ravishing desire by barely contain-able, savage black men. Look up the Equal Justice Initiative report to see how many lynchings were executed for reasons related to sexual assault charges purportedly involving white women in addition to misinformed or petty reasons. See <*http://www.eji.org/files/EJI%20Lynching%20in%20America%20SUMMARY.pdf*> for a report summary.

# CRITICAL QUESTIONS

99) **First consider:** Further, what do you think about a photograph found at the national chain, Joe's Crab Shack, entitled "Lynching of Henry Smith, Paris, Texas, 1893" (see <*https://www.washingtonpost.com/news/morn-ing-mix/wp/2016/03/11/this-photo-of-a-black-mans-public-hanging-decorated-a-joes-crab-shack-table/*>)? Not only was the real death of two individuals on display (potentially enough for one to lose an appe-tite), but it was also revised with a caption containing a "joke" (e.g., "All I said was that I wanted the gumbo!"). What can the chain possibly do to repair the damage done? Or is the damage too abstract to address? What does this say about the black image in the white mind?

100) **Then contemplate:** Look at a modern mainstream Hollywood movie, such as *Get Hard*, featuring Kevin Hart and Will Ferrell. How many of the jokes are specifically race related? How much of the humor hearkens back to the minstrel humor of old?

## B. The era of segregation constituted much more than mere restrictions on water fountains and park benches as commonly depicted.

# CRITICAL CONCEPTS

101) *Coming of Age in Mississippi*, **an autobiography of civil rights activist Anne Moody**

The manuscript provides a rare opportunity to "time travel" and see through the eyes of a child what life was like growing up black, poor, and female in a segregated society. The account reads like gripping fiction but is entirely painful and real. This helps us resist the temptation to casually dismiss racism as limited to ugly acts like slavery only. Even though Anne is not whipped like a slave, the careful reader will see how she is equally as scarred if not more so since there is this constant distraction in her mind about living as a "free" person within a "free" society.

102) **Thomas Hovendon**

An Irish-American teacher and artist who painted realistic quiet family scenes, narrative subjects, and often depicted African Americans. He painted *Breaking Home Ties*, which shows the reality facing many Americans as many migrated from the farms to the city during the busy period of urbanization in efforts to improve their fortunes. As the southern economy remained crippled in the aftermath of enslavement's dismantling in concert with technological advances (e.g., Eli Whitney's cotton gin), many rural residents felt pressure to seek out a better claim for the American Dream within the larger urbanized areas. Many members of the younger generation decided to try their (Horatio Alger) luck by going to the urban areas due to the worsening plight of the farmer. During the period 1870–1920, 11 million Americans deserted farms for cities. Ironically, large investments in farm machinery doubled wheat and cotton output, further placing the "free labor" notion of independence and opportunity for social mobility under challenge.

103) *Laissez faire*

The theory or system of government that upholds the autonomous character of the economic order, believing that government should intervene

*Introduction to African-American Studies*

as little as possible in the direction of economic affairs. This policy was detrimental to blacks who saw government largess truncated on their behalf with only a twelve-year reconstruction period. The notion that all citizens were considered to operate on a level playing field and that no one required special assistance from the government fueled the popularity of this laissez faire economic situation, whereupon the federal and state governments were no longer responsible for ensuring black success. A francophone term, *laissez faire* means "hands off," a concept that supported early nineteenth-century republicanism, where it was more popular to espouse that those who made the wealth should directly enjoy its fruits within a democratically self-governed system. The notion of an activist federal government was discredited in the eyes of many as government was seen by many as more ineffectual and "corrupt" than the private sector. The idea of "laissez faire" thus gained ground at precisely the moment when industrialization began to accelerate.

## 104) Horatio Alger myth

Horatio Alger wrote over 100 books for boys, the first, *Ragged Dick*, being published in 1867. By leading exemplary lives, struggling valiantly against poverty and adversity, Alger's heroes gain wealth and honor. His works were all extremely popular in supporting the idea that one's fortune and rise in social standing was only limited by how hard they wished to work. The Horatio Alger myth is one of the fundamental tenets of the American Dream—the idea that anyone can be anything they want, just so long as they work hard for it.[1]

© neftali/Shutterstock.com

### 105) Mary Church Terrell

She became active in the suffragist movement, founding the Colored Women's League in 1892. In 1896 this club merged with the National Federation of Afro-American Women to become the National Federation of Colored Women, and Church Terrell was elected its first president. In 1895 she became the first African American woman appointed to the District of Columbia Board of Education. A charter member of the NAACP, she was a popular lecturer on equal rights for women and blacks and served as a delegate at various international women's rights congresses. Terrell was often critical of her white female colleagues, being one of the first to highlight the difficulty of identifying as both as female and as black. Terrell's rhetoric echoed a preeminent black female voice several years prior, Sojourner Truth who incredulously inquired of her white female colleagues, "arn't I a woman?" Legal scholar Kimberlé Crenshaw many years after Terrell and Truth fostered the concept of intersectionality—the idea that only black-centered remedies and neither female-centered remedies as recognized by law adequately recognize the unique dilemma of being both.

## CRITICAL QUESTS

### 106) Objective: *To understand the impact of Robber Barons*

Robber Barons were large corporate magnates (e.g., J.P. Morgan, Dale Carnegie, John D. Rockefeller, Samuel P. Chase) who amassed great personal wealth and influence through aggressive business tactics. Between 1882 and 1892, millions of people were mobilizing against monopolies and demanding greater democracy. These corporate magnates continued to thrive economically amidst financially difficult times and increasing labor-capital conflict. For instance, with the Panic of 1893, 491 banks failed along with 15,000 businesses. Despite the Robber Barons' experience differing dramatically from the average citizen and in spite of the fact that many of their monopolizing tactics exploited many of the poor and vulnerable, their names still live on as clear-cut examples of Horatio Alger success or the American Dream. To this extent, look up more recent manifestations of this homage. In particular, what did you find out about successful rapper and international celebrity Jay Z's connection to Roc-A-Fella Records label he help co-found in 1996? Does "Roc-A-Fella" pay homage to the Robber Baron name "Rockefeller"? If so, why?

107) **Objective:** *To understand how many people left the farm for the city*
Look up statistics of migration from the farms to the inner cities. Are any of these statistics aggregated for race? Tenets of early nineteenth-century republicanism (e.g., individual autonomy, economic self-sufficiency, ownership of the means of one's livelihood, and opportunity for upward social mobility) began to erode in the rural areas as it became harder to eke out a living with lowering product sales and rising labor costs. For instance, in the 1870s, cotton prices were as high as twelve cents a pound; in the 1890s, prices plummeted to only six cents a pound. If such economic conditions proved difficult for average whites, the onus only increased for those who were visibly identifiable as nonwhite individuals. Given the historical legacy of nonwhites being underresourced, what was the likelihood of blacks successfully pursuing the Horatio Alger narrative of moving toward the "big city" and finding work? What type of skills would they possess? What institutional barriers would they have to hurdle? How much of racism was still a factor at this point in time? The Homestead Act of 1862 was another push factor.

108) **Objective:** *To find how hard life was as a domestic worker*
Look up what percentage of domestic workers were black around 1920–1940. Can you find information on how many were sexually exploited? Little sympathy was given to domestic workers specifically, likely because working conditions for whites postenslavement were not easy generally. Robber Barons as employers were growing economically and politically, which meant that workers often lacked clear legal rights toward organizing and striking. Further, in reflecting back on Anne Moody's early life, she too, worked as a domestic during her formative teenage years—and not just because she desired extra disposable income for sweet delights after school, but because her family needed the extra income to survive. How did Moody "come of age," especially when considering modern mainstream depictions of (white) Americans enjoying the awkward "coming of age" phase in a more glamorized fashion (*<http://thoughtcatalog.com/lance-pauker/2013/09/the-25-best-coming-of-age-movies-in-the-last-25-years/>*)?

# CRITICAL QUESTIONS

109) **First consider:** Who does the 2011 movie *The Help* help? Did white female author Kathryn Stockett have black women in mind as her target audience? If not, then who?

110) **Then contemplate:** What would Anne Moody think of the movie *The Help* today? The movie ends with the two principal black characters in main outfits while the white author who "helped" them left for her new career in New York. Would Moody find this to be cathartic? Redeeming? Inspiring? Wholesome? Entertaining?

## C. Leading thinkers were divided upon strategies to best combat the suppressive conditions of Jim Crow.

# CRITICAL CONCEPTS

© Everett Historical/Shutterstock.com

111)     **Booker T. Washington**
Washington was an author, educator, orator, philanthropist, and, from 1895 until his death in 1915, the most famous U.S. African American. The tiny school he founded in Tuskegee, Alabama, in 1881 is now Tuskegee University, an institution that currently enrolls more than 3,000 students. The most famous of the several books he authored, coauthored, or edited during his lifetime, *Up from Slavery* (1901), has become a classic of American autobiography. His foremost critic was African American writer and intellectual W.E.B. Du Bois for having been an "accommodationist": one who, in order to gain a measure of economic success

for African Americans in the former slave states, accepted segregation and refused to speak out loudly in favor of other forms of advancement, namely the pursuit of full legal, political, and social equality. Booker T. Washington is likely most famous for his 1895 "Atlanta Compromise" speech, whereupon he stated on social matters, blacks and whites could remain "separate as the fingers on a hand, yet one as the hand in all things essential to mutual progress." Many southern whites afterward embraced Washington as they perceived him to advocate for self-segregation without contesting the white man's "place" above him in society. Washington shrewdly used such patronage to finance the creation and operation of a black institution still in existence today.

## 112) W.E.B. DuBois

Scholar and political activist W.E.B. Du Bois helped found the National Association for the Advancement of Colored People (NAACP). DuBois attended Harvard University and in 1895 became the first African American to receive a Ph.D. degree from this Ivy League standard bearer. DuBois is likely best known for his seminal work, *The Souls of Black Folk,* wherein he advances the theory of the "talented tenth," or the idea that the best and the brightest of African Americans would be able to use education as a lever to extricate themselves and the whole of the black community out of doldrums and into the elite circles of white existence. To this point, DuBois help found the National Association for the Advancement of Colored People in 1909, which became an organization promoting progress and social equality for blacks and eventually launched the successful legal strategy that dismantled Jim Crow, courtesy of the NAACP Legal Defense Fund. Frustrated with the failure of his own Horatio Alger narrative, DuBois spent his last years as a citizen of Ghana.

## 113) Twoness

The concept of twoness and double-consciousness by W.E.B. DuBois suggested an irrational force and the emergence of a dual and split personality entombed in one physical body. The dual and split nature of this consciousness suggested that what was in play was the existence of a "true" and genuine self, which could be contrasted to a self that was "false" and inauthentic in being asked to be both "African" and "American." Said DuBois in *Souls of Black Folk*:

> After the Egyptian and Indian, the Greek and Roman, the Teuton and Mongolian, the Negro is a sort of seventh son, born with a veil, and gifted with second-sight in this American world,—a world which yields him no true self-conscious-

ness, but only lets him see himself through the revelation of the other world. It is a peculiar sensation, this double-consciousness, this sense of always looking at one's self through the eyes of others, of measuring one's soul by the tape of a world that looks on in amused contempt and pity. One ever feels his two-ness,—an American, a Negro; two souls, two thoughts, two unreconciled strivings; two warring ideals in one dark body, whose dogged strength alone keeps it from being torn asunder.

### 114) Jane Addams

Addams help usher in the Progressive Era with the establishment of the Hull House settlement house for incoming immigrants in Chicago in 1889 with Gates Starr. The Hull House was praised for providing key resources to immigrants to help them properly transition into valuable contributors within the American economy. The Hull House was criticized for merely conditioning individuals to be compliant, obedient, and dutiful laborers at their own expense. Additionally, the Hull House focused primarily upon white European immigrants. Efforts of the Hull House and other institutions also helped white immigrants become white Americans while full black citizenship was still at issue. Addams's efforts came on the heels of publicly stated fears of immigrant hordes. To this extent, the American Protective Association (APA) was founded in 1887 in Iowa by Henry Bowers and by 1895 had 100,000 members in at least eleven states (Wisconsin, Missouri, Illinois, Kansas, Ohio, Michigan, New York, Pennsylvania, Massachusetts, Connecticut, and Rhode Island). The APA was united by Anti-Catholic and anti-Semitic biases and called for immigration restriction. Addams thus represented a new wave of Progressive thought, influenced by social Darwinism and scientific racism otherwise stylized as the "White Man's Burden," or responsibility for civilizing the less civilized. This burden corresponded with an overriding desire for "social justice" and quest for efficiency. Addams and other Progressives believed that corporate capitalism could be reformed and that efforts to overturn it were dangerous.

### 115) Tom Watson

A southern Populist who was elected to the U.S. Congress from Georgia in 1890, made one of the strongest cases for an alliance of black and white farmers. Yet, Watson called for a strategic political alliance, not a fully integrated society, and his commitment to interracialism did not survive

*Introduction to African-American Studies*

the defeat of the Populist movement. Before the Populists were defeated, Tom Watson offered on the racial divide: "You are made to hate each other because on that hatred is rested the keystone of the arch of financial despotism." On the need for interracial solidarity, Watson also stated, "The colored tenant is in the same boat with the white tenant, the colored laborer with the white laborer... the accident of color makes no difference in the interests of farmers, croppers, and laborers." After the turn of the century, Watson led efforts to disenfranchise African Americans, publishing demagogic attacks on them as well as on Catholics and Jews.

# CRITICAL QUESTS

116) **Objective:** *To research the leading schools of thought for black progress*
As Fredrickson pointed out many different schools of thought among whites over how to handle blacks, naturally, there was plenty of debate within the African American community about how to best combat racial oppression. The two leading schools of thought were to either (a) work hard on practical jobs and shun integration or (b) integrate and compete for the highest intellectual positions of influence. Obviously, there is no "right" answer, but read their works and decide with whom you would have cast your lot were you alive then.
   • "The Negro in the New World," Booker T. Washington, *Journal of the Royal African Society*, Vol. 10, No. 38 (Jan., 1911), pp. 173-178.
   • "The Development of a People," W. E. B. DuBois, *International Journal of Ethics*, Vol. 14, No. 3 (Apr., 1904), pp. 292-311.

117) **Objective:** *To find the difficulty in choosing a strategy*
Look up the poem, "Booker T and WEB" by Dudley Randall. This poem is significant because it perfectly encapsulates the tension between Booker T. Washington and Dr. DuBois and their two schools of thought. After reading the poem, which of the two does the poet seem to favor? Who's argument/platform do you find more persuasive?

| Booker T. Washington | W.E.B. DuBois |
|---|---|
| Former slave-turned educator | Harvard Ph.D. |
| The Hampton Institute (Tuskegee) | The Niagara Movement (NAACP) |
| Vocational education | "The Talented Tenth" |
| Political, not social equality | Social AND political equality |

118) **Objective:** *To appreciate the political complexity of the eight-hour work day*
Look up rhetoric surrounding the eight-hour work day. What do you make of literature demanding that white workers are not to be treated like "slaves" now that the free market economy dictates that everyone must work for their own living. Did Robber Barons exploit whites in the same manner as white plantation workers exploited enslaved blacks? What are similarities and differences?

## CRITICAL QUESTIONS

119) **First consider:** Woodrow Wilson did not own slaves like previous presidents did. Owner of a unique career, Wilson obtained his Ph.D. from Johns Hopkins in 1883, served as university president of Ivy League Princeton University from 1902–1910, and served as governor of New Jersey from 1910–1912 before assuming the Presidency of the United States of America. Yet, he did host "The Birth of a Nation" screening and did not oppose the suggestion of segregating the federal workforce by his postmaster Albert Burleson in 1913. Where do these acts place Wilson's legacy? The Princeton University board of trustees wrestled with this issue as recent as April 2016, when they voted to keep his name on school buildings despite his checkered past on race relations (see *<http://www.npr.org/sections/thetwo-way/2016/04/04/472985937/princeton-will-keep-woodrow-wilsons-name-on-school-buildings>*).

120) **Then contemplate:** Once blacks were "free" to compete with whites for resources within the free market economy, what happened to the black image within the white mind?

## Footnotes:

[1] "The Horatio Alger myth has become emblematic of the American Dream." Art Silverblatt, Jane Ferry, Barbara Finan. Approaches to Media Literacy: A Handbook. New York: Routledge, 2009, p. 205.

# module 5

# BLACK RENAISSANCE

*"Despite existing social challenges, the worst in American society brought out some of the best in African American society."*

## PRIMARY IDEAS TO BEAR IN MIND:

A. The period of black renaissance was of vital importance to African Americans because it was a collective counter to the disparaged black image.

B. Through art and poetry, music and movement, blacks occupied a new space whereupon their inner thoughts and ideas had value.

C. Yet, blacks tread the tensions of romantic racialism all over again where they run the danger of only being seen as entertainers.

A. The period of black renaissance was of vital importance to African Americans because it was a collective counter to the disparaged black image.

## CRITICAL CONCEPTS

121) **Black renaissance**

Otherwise known as the "Harlem Renaissance," this was a dynamic era wherein many blacks showcased intelligent, artistic talents that they were presumed not to possess. We see an explosion of blacks with music (jazz), dancing, song, and poetry during the 1920s. This renaissance was a direct counternarrative to popularized mainstream images that disparaged black existence in the aftermath of enslavement and failed Reconstruction.

122) *Birth of a Nation*

A 1915 mainstream movie release that prominently featured the vigilante group, Ku Klux Klan. The movie is still shown in film schools across the country, because it is known as a cinematic innovator or the unofficial progenitor of the modern mainstream movie. Yet, the content indisputably did not portray blacks in a flattering light; it was quite the opposite. Many of the "black" characters in the movie were portrayed by whites in blackface.

123) **The Big City**

Urbanization took hold of the nation with massive migration from rural, farm areas to metropolitan areas during the period 1870–1900. Examples of this vibrant growth include New Orleans, which experienced population growth of 100% during this period; Buffalo, 300%; Chicago 500%. By the turn of the century (1900), 40% of Americans lived in cities and New York City's population alone (3.5 million) was equal to the entire U.S. urban population of 1850. The urbanization was also fueled in part by massive immigration, which led to dense concentrations of immigrant groups in potentially difficult-to-assimilate enclaves. Italian, Irish, and Jewish immigrants mostly started off ostracized in lower income neighborhoods called "ghettoes," but were later able to move out of such locales. Currently, the term *ghetto* is a quasi-intractable term primarily associated with lower income African American neighborhoods and the lifestyle/culture associated with such living conditions.

124) **Harlem**

A neighborhood in the Manhattan section of New York City, originally settled by Dutch but eventually populated by blacks migrating north. While blacks were originally the minority, Harlem quickly became known as a place for black settlement having gone from 10% black to 70% black in a mere two-decade period from 1910 to 1930. Black migration was sustained with jobs supplied with the WWI effort, fueling a window of temporary prosperity allowing for blacks to find time to express themselves in new artistic ways through the Harlem renaissance. Yet, once job growth curtailed in the aftermath of the Depression, Harlem became synonymous with the prototypical black "ghetto" overrun with crime and infested with drugs. Given the neighborhood's sound architectural foundation and proximity to New York's central business district, Harlem has reemerged as an attractive locale and is currently a prime example of gentrification at work with only a 40% black population.

125) **Flapper**

© Gorbash Varvara/Shutterstock.com

This term symbolized the changing gender roles in society revolving around new attitudes of sexual behavior. It typically represented a woman who was "free" to wear her hair short and her hemlines above the knee. Flappers were seen as cultural rebels who rejected Victorian and Puritanical tastes that emphasized female modesty and deference, most especially in the presence of men. At the same time mostly white women were seeking liberation, many black women continued to live lives mostly shaped by domestic work. In other words, black women were busy cleaning homes and watching the children of white women while (white) flappers were free to explore their existence.

# CRITICAL QUESTS

126) **Objective:** *To understand the black image in the black mind*

Look up selected portraits by Gordon Parks at the U.S. Library of Congress to see how he showcased early black images (*<http://www.loc.gov/pictures/search/?q=gordon%20parks&co=fsa>*). What themes are present and consistent?

127) **Objective:** *To understand effects of immigration upon the American economy*

All countries experience immigration. However, American immigration is unique in that it was more voluminous, more diverse, and more continuous than immigration experienced by other industrializing societies. Immigration at the turn of the twenty-first century distinctly transformed the American social structure with the emergence of a new corporate elite that strove to rise above proletarianization.

128) **Objective:** *To understand the resurgence of the KKK*

After originally sprouting immediately after the Civil War in 1866, the KKK experienced a revival during the 1920s, having peaked in membership at 4 million.[1] Their antimodern impulses were to reverse Progressive era trends as they continued their search for cultural purity. New KKK members bonded around anti-immigrant feeling and immigration restriction and continuing racial conflict. The KKK was mainstream, having marched on Pennsylvania Avenue in Washington, D.C., in 1926. Outnumbered and outgunned, most blacks did not retaliate against them, as the Klan was rarely active where blacks were the majority and prepared to defend themselves. The Klan usually attacked those who could not defend themselves.

© Everett Historical/Shutterstock.com

# CRITICAL QUESTIONS

129) **First consider:** What was the U.S. relationship with labor? Even whites had contentious relationships with their employers. Consider early American federal law that favored corporate rights and immunities and local laws restricting labor unions where the legal right to organize were not generally protected. Additionally, "Conspiracy laws" still occasionally were used to prosecute unions that did strike. Courts freely issued injunctions against strikers, and the U.S. army, state militias, and police forces repeatedly were used against strikers. How then did this environment complicate the ascent of would-be black aspirants of the American Dream?

130) **Then contemplate:** Watch the clip from *Birth of a Nation* (<*http://www. youtube.com/watch?v=UYCaob7MDA8*>). Is Negrophobia still at large?

## B. Through art and poetry, music and movement, blacks occupied a new space whereupon their inner thoughts and ideas had value.

# CRITICAL CONCEPTS

131) **Langston Hughes**
Arguably, one of the most famous black poets during this time was Langston Hughes. Known for such works as "Dream Deferred," "Ku Klux," "Minstrel Man," "I, Too, Sing America," Langston is credited with articulating the depths and contours of the black experience with dignity, charm, and grace not seen since the early arrival of enslaved Africans.

132) **"Strange Fruit"**
The name of a somber song by famous jazz songstress Billie Holiday. "Strange Fruit" told the story of a produce that had "bulging eyes," "twisted lips," and "blood on leaves." An allegory for lynching, this was a daring act of protest where Holiday heightened awareness by performing the song for mostly white audiences.

133) **Fordism**
The mass production/consumption system dynamics named after Henry Ford who pioneered an innovative and cost-efficient strategy in manufacturing with his Model T Ford, which debuted in 1914. Rather than have trained artisans and experts labor relentlessly over one product at a time, increasing the time and cost of the product's production, Ford took the entire assembly process and compartmentalized it into smaller parts

so that unskilled workers could simply execute their one task repeatedly within an assembly line en route to a finished product.

134) **Jazz**

This explosion of new sound emphasized and encouraged creativity, even extemporaneous activity as artists would "riff," or improvise sound with their instrument within a similar key of the original song composed. Jazz then expanded to represent a cultural style comprising manner of speech, dress, and movement. Yet, this cultural development, largely fueled by incoming black migrants from rural areas looking to make their mark within urban enclaves, was roundly criticized at the time: "The music is sensuous, the embracing of partners is absolutely indecent; and the motions are such as may not be described in a family newspaper" (*Cincinnati Catholic Herald*).

135) **Madame C.J. Walker**

The first female millionaire, let alone black female millionaire in the United States. Walker gained her fortune primarily through the manufacturing and retail of black hair care products. Walker seized upon an opportunity overlooked by larger corporate interests that primarily tailored their products and marketing toward white customers only.

## CRITICAL QUESTS

136) **Objective:** *To understand the genius of Langston Hughes*

First, ask yourself if you have ever heard of Hughes before. Then ask your parents. Then ask yourself again, why not? At any rate, look at how he poignantly captures the emotion of the time with the precision of a camera with his poem "Go Slow" (<*http://www.historyisaweapon.com/defcon1/langston.html*>). How does his choice of words help you visualize the sentiment shared at the time?. Further, consider the poem, "As I Grew Older" by Langston Hughes.

137) **Objective:** *To understand the proliferation of jazz today*

Look up "smooth jazz" today. What type of artists do you find? How did jazz, which originally started off as an ostracized form of black music from a group of people who were isolated and excluded from society over a few decades, morph into an American invention that includes all sectors of society?

138) **Objective:** *To find how contentious the new economy was still*
Look up early strike history. How many strikes were settled by violence? What does the presence of violence suggest about a democratic republic?

## CRITICAL QUESTIONS

139) **First consider:** Jamaican immigrant Marcus Garvey during this time advocated a radical solution for black Americans—namely, that members of his Universal Negro Improvement Association could take his Black Star Line ocean liner and immigrate out of the country entirely. The plan failed when Garvey was jailed and later deported for improperly using the U.S. mail system to solicit funds. Was Garvey's idea of colonization revolutionary and isolationist? Or was it merely reminiscent of what early European settlers did centuries earlier?

140) **Then contemplate:** Is "renaissance" an appropriate term to use? What does it mean that most famous African American figures of that era were largely limited to sports/entertainment? Are there traces of Romantic Racialism at play here?
- Nicholas Brothers
- Gertrude "Ma" Rainey
- Jack Johnson
- C.J. Walker
- Jelly Roll Morton
- Paul Robeson
- Bill Pickett
- Andrew "Rube" Foster
- Jesse Owens
- Joe Louis

## C. Yet, blacks tread the tensions of romantic racialism all over again where they run the danger of only being seen as entertainers.

## CRITICAL CONCEPTS

141) *Stormy Weather*
An incredible example of human ingenuity, the infamous "staircase scene" will likely never be duplicated. Such physical gifts demonstrated by tap dancing legends, the Nicholas Brothers were misinterpreted as the

black performer who "knows their place" as entertainers within a white gaze. Instead, their incomparable feat must be understood as a defiant declaration of humanity—the intelligence, sophistication, and bravura to even attempt the staircase scene is evidence of existence that cannot be limited to house servants and bar maids.

**142) Social Darwinism**

Social Darwinism was fueled by Horatio Alger's rags-to-riches ethic that presumed success only required hard work, virtue, and a little luck. In addition, success required an absence of racism, as overt racism was still a significant barrier to entry of the labor force. As more individuals flooded the densely populated cities, transitioning from farmer/peasant to a wage-worker or from independent artisan to wage worker laboring for others, between 1890 and 1910, African Americans experienced a loss of political and economic power unlike anything experienced by any other group (with the exception of Native Americans). For the lack of black success was presumed to be explained by inferior effort, not superior exclusion.

**143) Hollywood**

With more leisure time on the hands of more workers in more densely populated areas, movies became more important to society. Movie attendance averaged an eye-popping 80 million a week by 1930. Hollywood moguls effectively fueled fantasies with a cost-effective model. As opposed to a successful play that requires live actors to repeat their performances multiple times in different cities, one movie can be distributed for replay multiple times. While mostly fictional movies were most popular in theaters, movies nonetheless began to both reflect and reinforce mainstream culture.

**144) *The Jazz Singer***

In 1927, *The Jazz Singer* made cinematic history by becoming the first movie with audio sound synched with the visual images shown on screen. Starring Jewish actor Al Jolson, the song was about Jolson rejecting his devoutly religious immigrant parentage and opting for a career in show business rather than become a cantor in the synagogue. The movie's climactic scene features Jolson donning blackface to sing the song "Mammy."

**145) Lincoln Theodore Monroe Andrew Perry**

A black minstrel performer in early American film, Perry was better known by his stage name, "Steppin Fetchit." Perry did not don blackface like other white actors, but he nonetheless exaggerated his actions, motions, and speech to appear as a caricature of himself with virtually all jokes made at his characters' expense. To the chagrin of black audiences, he was loved by white audiences and leveraged his notoriety toward becoming one of the first known black millionaires.

## CRITICAL QUESTS

146) **Objective:** *To research #oscarssowhite and compare to 1939*
What has changed? Hattie McDaniel won the first Academy Award for any nonwhite person for playing Mammy in *Gone with the Wind*. How has nonwhite inclusion in this hallowed club changed over the years changed?

147) **Objective:** *To find the impact of early images*
In view of the fact that 80 million were viewing the movies weekly in this era, look up what percentage of 80 million was the nation's population? Think about how there are more options for entertainment currently, and how with fewer options at the time such images might have played upon unsuspecting members of society.

148) **Objective:** *To appreciate how difficult the "staircase scene" was to achieve in real life*
As an example of the black renaissance in motion, check out the following YouTube clip as one mere example (*<http://www.youtube.com/watch?v=zBb9hTyLjfM>*) . Well, more accurately, it is a dance number by the Nicholas Brothers that is quite impressive. Ask yourself, what does their physical feat perhaps suggest about their intellectual capacity? How might the proliferation of blacks in the arts continue to underscore notions of romantic racialism?

## CRITICAL QUESTIONS

149) **First consider:** Could Steppin Fetchit have achieved mainstream success any other way at that time? In other words, could the actor Perry have created a different persona, a stronger, more competent image of a black male that would have been widely received and patronized just as strongly?

150) **Then contemplate:** How has the black image in the white mind changed over time from enslavement to Jim Crow?

## Footnotes:

[1]  "By 1925 total Ku Klux Klan membership was about 4 million." Lisa Klobuchar. *1963 Birmingham Church Bombing: The Ku Klux Klan's History of Terror.* Mankato, MN: Compass Point Books, 2009.

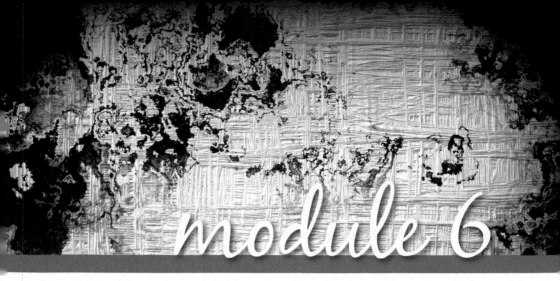

# module 6

# GREAT MIGRATION

---

*"Key period that helps explain current demographic living patterns, particularly in large, metropolitan urban areas; many African Americans left the south for the 'big city' in search of the American Dream."*

---

## PRIMARY IDEAS TO BEAR IN MIND:

A. The great migration for blacks started roughly around World War I and peaked during the World War II years. Many push and pull factors were involved.

B. Between the two World Wars, in 1929, the United States experienced the start of the Great Depression; if times were hard for whites, one can only imagine the impact upon blacks.

C. The U.S. federal government responded with one of the largest welfare programs ever to help all citizens, although mostly white citizens benefitted.

**A. The great migration for blacks started roughly around World War I and peaked during the World War II years. Many push and pull factors were involved.**

## CRITICAL CONCEPTS

151) **Great Migration**

A massive transfer of human capital from economically depressed and politically suppressive areas in the South up toward northern or midwestern metropolises by African Americans. Pushing blacks away was an increasingly stagnant southern agrarian economy deeply rooted (no pun intended) in sharecropping with many landowners reluctant to invest in cutting-edge technology. Domestic terrorism (e.g., vigilantism, KKK, Jim Crow) was also a strong push factor. Pulling blacks to northern cities was the lure of the Horatio Alger myth—the idea that if one merely works hard, one can make it.

152) **Boll weevil**

The boll weevil was a vermin-based plague that destroyed cotton from Mexico to the Carolinas. With many crops devastated in Mississippi and Alabama in 1915, many black sharecroppers and laborers had little recourse in the South for economic survival. In effect this small vermin had a large impact upon America's cultural development.

153) **World War I**

With labor shortages induced by the advent of WWI in industry and manufacturing, this war also put a halt on European immigration, eliminating a cheap source of labor, increasing the value of black labor. WWI thus provided newfound jobs for blacks in northern factories processing large orders for weaponry domestically and abroad. This development hearkens back indirectly to the dynamic demonstrated in the Civil War where military conflict provided a window of opportunity for blacks to "prove" their usefulness in sectors of society normally restricted from black participation

154) **Sen. James K. Vardaman**

A Mississippi senator who encapsulated the antipathy blacks faced within public circles by prominent whites well after the era of enslavement ended. Vardaman was so angry over conservative, nationally known educator Booker T. Washington having dinner with President Theodore Roosevelt at the White House that he proclaimed the White House was "so saturated with the odor of the nigger that the rats have taken refuge in the stable."

*Introduction to African-American Studies*

155) **"Memorial Day Massacre"**

An unfortunate representation of violent labor conflict. In Chicago 1937, labor union membership was rising, particularly for immigrant laborers and other low-wage workers who wanted more accelerated paths toward the American Dream. Here, thugs were hired by company representatives to "disrupt" protests that disrupted production resulting in fatalities.

# CRITICAL QUESTS

156) **Objective:** *To understand the racial nature of upward mobility*

Was this concept true for all blacks? Look up "Horatio Alger" stories to see what you come up with and ask yourself whether it was possible to see blacks experience that type of upward mobility back then, and if not, why not. Compare black upward mobility to that of other groups initially ostracized and targeted for their identity, such as Jewish immigrants. Shelly Tenenbaum. "Jewish Immigrants and American Capitalism, 1880–1920 (review)." *Journal of Interdisciplinary History* 41(2) (2010): 314-315. Project MUSE. Web. 25 Jan. 2013. <*http://muse.jhu.edu/*>

157) **Objective:** *To understand northern poverty*

Many blacks soon learned that paradise in the North was hard to earn. Look up the images in "Alley Life in Washington" by Bochert and see what you think.[1]

158) **Objective:** *To understand the subjugated black image in the white mind*

Zieger notes that in "the 1930s and 1940s, films and radio shows often portrayed black domestic workers in idealized fashion. Characters such as Mammy, played by Hattie McDaniel in *Gone with the Wind* and Rochester, played by Eddie Anderson on the *Jack Benny Program*, appeared as respected members of white employers' families. Their spunkiness, sagacity, and common sense contrasted with the white stars' ineptitude and pretensions; viewers and listeners were encouraged to applaud their insouciance and down-to-earth wisdom. In reality, however, domestic workers' female employers often treated them harshly, and the culture of white males encouraged sexual exploitation. Chiseling on wage payments was commonplace with employers attempting to substitute leftover food and cast-off clothing for agreed-upon monetary wages. Employers expected household servants to be available at short notice, whatever their own families' needs" (Zieger, *For Jobs and Freedom*, p. 146). Unlike the movie *The Help*, which was a fictional account written by a white woman several decades later, see how many popular first-person accounts you can find at that moment in time.

## CRITICAL QUESTIONS

159) **First consider:** What was the tangible social, economic, and political value to whiteness (at least by default of cost of being black)? Historian David Roediger in his research asserts that white workers made a deal to receive public and psychological "wage of whiteness" in return for accepting substantial elite political-economic dominance. Do you agree or disagree? Why or why not?

160) **Then contemplate:** WWI conditions for African American soldiers were reminiscent of conditions faced during the Civil War. Meaning, black troops openly suffered discrimination, abuse, and neglect. They drilled with picks and shovels as opposed to being "trusted" with real rifles. They lived in tents with no floors, no blankets, or no bathing facilities through cold winters. White soldiers would not salute black superiors, and black officers were denied admission to officer clubs. Black soldiers mostly fulfilled grunt work positions such as stevedores, road construction, cooks, and bakers. Black troops even went abroad for the war effort and returned to America on segregated ships. Does history repeat itself?

## B. Between the two World Wars, in 1929, the United States experienced the start of the Great Depression; if times were hard for whites, one can only imagine the impact upon blacks.

## CRITICAL CONCEPTS

161) **Black poverty**
Consider, if many whites were destitute and were struggling for survival, then practically, what did that mean for African Americans who socially, politically, and economically were below or behind whites by virtually any metric? Many social programs (e.g., Social Security) were started in the aftermath of the Great Depression as a means for the country to help those in need so that the country could remain an overall strong country. Yet, these programs did little to alleviate the economic suffering common to many black citizens at the time.

162) **Social Security Act**
Programs administered by states (unemployment and ADC) could be severely underfunded. Initial retirement payments tended to be low (as low
as $10 a month). Programs tended to have a deflationary impact on the
economy early on. Farm workers, domestic workers, and civil servants
were not covered, which meant that a significant proportion of "black
and brown" workers did not benefit from this social program designed to
invest within one's future.

163) **Fireside Chats**
In the wake of economic uncertainty, President Roosevelt held a series
of talks broadcast on national radio reassuring the public about the future economic prosperity of America. Dubbed "Fireside Chats," Roosevelt promised every American four freedoms: (1) freedom of speech, (2)
freedom of worship, (3) freedom of want, and (4) freedom from fear.

164) **New Deal Coalition**
In the wake of the Great Depression, the United States experienced a
changing role of government where a new philosophy of political economy was underway. A strengthened political alliance between the Democratic Party and organized labor, African Americans, and women's groups
emerged and organized to lobby for an eight-hour workday. For one of
the first times, "affinity" groups of leading African American organizations
had some recognized political moxie by endorsing FDR's reelection. Regarding women, FDR set up a Women's Division in the Democratic Party

165) **Brotherhood of Sleeping Car Porters**
A union headed by innovative strategist A. Philip Randolph. Randolph
successfully organized a vulnerable, yet visible workforce as black pullman porters were expected to be properly deferential to white patrons
traveling cross-country via train. While highly compensated in relation
to agricultural workers, pulllman porters were treated poorly on the job,
as if they were enslaved.[2]

# CRITICAL QUESTS

166) **Objective:** *To understand the struggle for black humanity*
Look up photographs by Carl Van Vetchen and describe what you see.

167) **Objective:** *To understand the black image in the white mind*
Look up WPA Slave Narratives in the Library of Congress. Some parts
are written to capture the vernacular of former black uneducated slaves.
Thus, while communicating the word "sure," the white author to most

accurately capture the sentiment of an unpolished southern accent would likely transcribe the word "sho." Yet, what if the same authors went to the Upper Northeast and were to transcribe unreadable Bostonian accents? How un/educated would normal whites appear?

168) **Objective:** *To find continuity over time*
In *Missouri v. Celia* (1855), a black slave was declared property without right to defense against a master's act of rape. Look up black domestic workers and reports of rape. How many were reported and acted upon? How was the black body respected?

## CRITICAL QUESTIONS

169) **First consider:** Who was pictured as suffering the most during the Depression? Look up the famous Depression era photograph "Face of Want" by Dorothea Lange before answering.

170) **Then contemplate:** What was the role/response of the government in the wake of financial crisis that affected whites? How different was the Social Security Administration from Reconstruction? The idea of a government-administered social safety net finally adopted in the United States contrasted with Reconstruction failures. Limitations of SSA (1935) included Old Age Pensions for those aged 65 or older to be funded by payroll contributions from workers and employers and matching funds to states to create:

- Unemployment Assurance
- Aid to Dependent Children

**C. The U.S. federal government responded with one of the largest welfare programs ever to help all citizens, although mostly white citizens benefitted.**

## CRITICAL CONCEPTS

171) **Unequal Poverty**
The only problem was, as you can imagine based upon the pattern we have discerned so far, while the Declaration of Independence informs us

that all citizens were created equal, seldom were they treated equal in this country. The Great Depression is directly related to the great migration, because when "finances are tight, people often fight." Thus, social tensions were already high as many whites were without resources. Scarcity of resources combined with heightened competition within more densely populated urban areas meant that blacks were often scapegoated and left out of the economic picture entirely. For example, according to the National Museum of Women's History, 52% of black women nationwide, and up to 90% in northern cities, were domestic servants (*<http://www.nwhm.org/online-exhibits/industry/7.htm>*).

172) **Wagner Act**

With the emergence of the "Second New Deal" in 1935, the National Labor Relations (Wagner) Act allowed workers to join unions and prohibited bargaining by "company unions." The Wagner Act also set up a National Labor Relations Board to oversee and enforce the law as a means to mitigate rising tensions between capital and labor.

173) **New Deal**

A massive incursion of social programming designed to help stabilize a floundering American economy in the aftermath of the Great Depression. By deciding to "invest" in America, large masses of Americans were able to find work that in turn helped the American economy rebound. Many of these programs were not labeled as welfare, even though they were designed to provide a service that individuals could not provide for themselves.

174) **American Families with Dependent Children**

AFDC was one such welfare program that provided food stamps to qualifying families that could be redeemed for food. While food stamps are commonly associated with blacks living within the proverbial "ghetto" today, they still are and always have been utilized by mostly whites.

175) **Works Progress Administration**

The WPA was arguably the largest New Deal job creation program yet. It funded job relief programs with an initial outlay of $5 billion. The WPA was headed by Harry Hopkins and for the eight-year period of 1935-42, the WPA would employ 8 million American workers.

## CRITICAL QUESTS

176) **Objective:** *To research work created by the New Deal*

Look up Hoover Dam and research which New Deal program sponsored this massive investment of human and economic capital. Did the investment pay off? Would Las Vegas, Nevada, be able to survive without the electricity generated by the dam?

177) **Objective:** *To find humor in the past*
In the movie *Bringing Down the House,* there is a "funny" scene where elderly white female billionaire, Mrs. Arness (Joan Plowright) belts out in song at the dinner table "Is Massa Gonna Sell Us Tomorrow?" To understand that this song spoke to a painful reality, look up the WPA slave narrative, "Jeff Davis used to camouflage his horse," by Levi D. Shelby, Jr.

178) **Objective:** *To appreciate early American protest*
A. Phillip Randolph threatened a national demonstration in Washington, D.C., 1941. President Roosevelt issued Executive Order 8802 creating the Fair Employment Practices Commission, 1941; and the March on Washington was called off. Look up the rhetoric employed at the time. Why did Randolph have so much leverage?

## CRITICAL QUESTIONS

179) **First consider:** Two major hits in American confidence were the Great Depression and WWI. How did America recover?

180) **Then contemplate:** Why did Roosevelt issue an Executive Order rather than pressure Congress to pass a bill legislating equal employment opportunities?

## Footnotes:

[1] James Borchert. *Alley Life in Washington: Family, Community, Religion, and Folklife in the City, 1850-1970.* 1980. Champaign, IL: University of Illinois Press.

[2] Consider how Pullman porter jobs were filled mostly by black males after the turn of the twentieth century who were expected to provide first-class, top rate service upon train cars to white patrons. Porters depended heavily upon tips and therefore appeared agreeable and obsequious. Additionally, founder George Pullman and management insisted that black porters provide service with a smile. To learn more, see: *<http://www.paulwagnerfilms.com/miles-of-smiles-about-porters/>.*

# module 7

# WWII AND BEYOND

---

*"Ironic period whereby even when fighting fascism abroad,
African Americans had to still fight racism domestically
(even within the "colorblind" armed services)."*

---

## PRIMARY IDEAS TO BEAR IN MIND:

A. The South was known for its virulent racism against blacks and the North was widely perceived as a more liberal alternative for migrating blacks.

B. World War II provided many blacks with newfound opportunities to interact with mainstream culture.

C. "Blood for water," or sacrificing one's body for the refreshing waters of democracy, was seen before in the Civil War and repeated again during WWII.

**A. The South was known for its virulent racism against blacks and the North was widely perceived as a more liberal alternative for migrating blacks.**

## CRITICAL CONCEPTS

181) **"The North"**

Typically, when thinking about "the North" versus "the South," the conventional wisdom is that the South was indisputably racist and that the North offered better opportunities while all other points on the map receive scant attention. If anything, consider how life could have been even MORE DIFFICULT for one moving to the North rather than remain in the South. Race riots in Detroit along with Mexican Zoot Suiters in 1943 speak to this conflict.

182) **Television**

Mass culture was televised for the first time by the box that changed the world. In 1940 only 10,000 televisions in United States with 6 television stations offered very limited programming; by 1960, 90% of households had a television, with 500 television stations offer all-day programming.

183) **John Maynard Keynes**

Keynes's *General Theory* (1936) espoused that deficit spending is appropriate in a depression. The "Multiplier Effect" dictated that unemployment in the nonfarm labor force decreased tremendously from 1929–1945. WWII provided excuse to spend—carrying over into cold war years. Keynes's theory symbolized the onset of new philosophy of political economy that focused primarily on demand side as opposed to supply side.

184) **Racial etiquette**

WWII was revolutionary to the extent that typical racial etiquette was challenged. Blacks were obedient and subservient, societal norms made white dominance clear. Blacks and whites could not shake hands, nor could blacks look directly into the eyes of Whites. Blacks stared at the ground when addressing whites, removed their hats in white presence, while the opposite did not occur. Blacks were called "boy," "auntie," "nigger" vs. "ma'am" or "sir" and had to enter establishments through the back versus the front door and were served last and could not try on clothing in stores. WWII exposed blacks to a world outside the socially, economically, and politically oppressive South.

**185) Redlining**
Along with racial covenants, both helped constrict social movement, even though it was not as overt and ugly as in the South. In the North, when selling real estate, agents literally would demarcate neighborhoods with red ink on maps indicating the areas they only would sell to black buyers. Racial covenants were legal agreements made by owners and buyers of property, binding them to a point of sale with whites only.

## CRITICAL QUESTS

**186) Objective:** *To understand the value of freedom*
In looking up Roosevelt's "Four Freedoms," research rhetoric by black newspapers that discuss or even celebrate these freedoms. Were these concepts fully explored by blacks as freely as whites?

**187) Objective:** *To understand how security has shaped America's identity*
With the passage of the National Security Act in 1947, how did America's identity globally and domestically change? The NSA created:
- New U.S. Department of Defense
- Central Intelligence Agency
- National Security Council
- Joint Chiefs of Staff

How did these developments affect blacks?

**188) Objective:** *To understand inconsistencies in federal policy*
How did the Federal Employee Loyalty Program square with the four freedoms? Executive Order 9835 (1947) allowed the screening of government workers for potential subversion; and accused workers did not have a right to face their accusers in hearings.

## CRITICAL QUESTIONS

**189) First Consider:** American exceptionalism really took off during the WWII period, meaning the philosophy of "what's good for America is good for the world." Do you agree?

**190) Then contemplate:** Interest Convergence, by noted legal theorist Derrick Bell, states that whites will only act for the interests of blacks to the extent it coincides with their interests. How might increased rights for blacks coincide with white interests during WWII?

**B. World War II provided many blacks with newfound opportunities to interact with mainstream culture.**

## CRITICAL CONCEPTS

191) **Dorie Miller**

Dorie Miller was a naval cook who, despite having no prior experience, took over a machine gun to fight attacking Japanese planes in the sky during the Pearl Harbor attack. Miller's bravery was lauded, but did not alter the Navy's policy of restricting black sailors to the kitchens and boiler rooms of Navy vessels. World War II broke out in Europe, September 1, 1939; and the U.S. entered the war, December 7, 1941 with the bombing of Pearl Harbor.

192) **Government Girls**

With the departure of many servicemen abroad, demand was increased for labor, opening the door to African Americans of both genders generally and white women specifically. Government Girls, or mostly white women, flooded the Washington, D.C. area pursuing a combination of the American Dream and the Dream American democracy. Government work also served as an entrée to clerical and subprofessional ranks for blacks otherwise lacking high school diplomas or college degrees. While such workers routinely suffered exclusion from comparable higher-paying, professionally ranked jobs in the private sector, the federal government provided broader access to clerical, semiprofessional, and in some cases, professional ones.

193) **Rosie the Riveter**

This graphic symbolized the new refined image of the American laborer, which was inclusive of both genders. Rosie was a white American woman complete with a headscarf and arm raised with bicep flexed. This image was in stark contrast to the "doll figure" that was too dainty to work. Rosie inspired millions and expanded the image range of femininity. All

*Introduction to African-American Studies*

Americans were counted upon to contribute to the war effort and this piece of positive propaganda still resonates within mainstream culture.

194) **WWII riots**

Similar to WWI, black soldiers did not experience a complete and total absence of racial tensions just because they were wearing official service uniforms. For example, in Port Chicago, July 1944, 320 people ended up dead after racial riots (mostly black victims) and black soldiers were later brought up on mutiny charges. At Fort Lawton in August 1944, 43 black soldiers were court-martialed based upon the Duncan Hunter National Defense Authorization Act. Lastly, at the Agana riots in December 1944, 2 people were found dead, and another was injured after more racial riots

195) **Tuskegee Airmen**

Black intelligence was presumed not to exist to the point were black males were deemed and declared incapable of operating expensive military equipment and thus were barred from flying airplanes during the war effort. This perception changed with a small group of airmen who hailed from Tuskegee, Alabama, and largely escorted bomber planes in Western Europe with an excellent service record.

## CRITICAL QUESTS

196) **Objective:** *To understand the racial phobias that existed during WWII*
Japanese American *citizens* were subjected to internment during the war effort since residence in California was deemed a threat to national security given California's "proximity" to Japan in the Pacific. Investigate rationales provided for Japanese internment and why not also Italian and German Americans on the East Coast, which is presumably closer to Western Europe?

197) **Objective:** *To understand how American loyalties changed over time*
Look up the 1943 poster entitled "Russian—this man is your friend!" versus the 1949 poster that incredulously asks, "Is this tomorrow: America under communism?" How does this compare to Thomas Nast and his two different depictions of African Americans during and after the Civil War?

198) **Objective:** *To find how black veterans were treated post-WWII*
Why would black veterans still face racial tensions after making the ultimate sacrifice of their own bodies? Look up this article and think about why there may have been resistance in recognizing black service: <*http://news.yahoo.com/u-honors-24-minority-veterans-world-war-two-224400047.html*>

# CRITICAL QUESTIONS

199) **First consider:** Black newspaper *Chicago Defender* exhorted the black community to move out of the South for better opportunities in the North. Were they right or wrong?

200) **Then contemplate:** America dropped the first ever atomic bombs in warfare on the two cities of Hiroshima and Nagasaki in August 1945. Given the targeted Japanese internment dynamic in the background, what was the rationale for only bombing Japan? America after all, was at war with several predominately white nations as well. Recall at the time, Italy was run by fascist Mussolini and Germany was run by Nazi Hitler. Was the bombing then "revenge" for Pearl Harbor? Or was it something else? Can you even list the other nations America was at war with?

## C. "Blood for water," or sacrificing one's body for the refreshing waters of democracy, was seen before in the Civil War and repeated again during WWII.

# CRITICAL CONCEPTS

201) **Double V**

"Double V" was a campaign created by black WWII veterans with one large capital V imposed over another V—the two Vs were to symbolize victory for Democracy against fascism abroad and victory against racism at home. This symbol is a telling but sobering reminder to the public that black veterans were American, but saw themselves as being differentiated in treatment from their white colleagues.

202) **GI Bill of Rights (1944)**

Colloquially known as the "GI Bill," it was a large welfare initiative specifically targeted toward former servicemen that allowed for college tuition to be paid for in full in payment and recognition of service provided to the armed forces. The GI Bill is directly responsible for the surge of college graduates entering the workforce thus able to command larger salaries. As part of the GI Bill, comprehensive healthcare was provided and the Veteran's Home Administration underwrote mortgages allowing for property acquisition.

203) **Baby Boom**

As America entered a new age of prosperity in the wake of WWII and increased production, more Americans were more settled, felt more secure in contrast to a decade and a half earlier with the Great Depression and Amer-

*Introduction to African-American Studies*

ica was the unquestioned leader of the free world. With all of these factors, many American families grew accounting for a "baby boom." The surge in population growth was another manifestation of the "people of plenty."

**204) White Flight**

As white families grew, concerns grew as to where was an appropriate place to raise a family in pursuit of the American Dream in peace. Two key factors fueled white flight: (1) The great migration of blacks from the South to mostly urban environments meant that over time, the "inner city" became synonymous with an undesirable area that was unsafe and unsavory and therefore unsuitable for habitation. (2) The post-WWII boom meant that many white families that benefitted economically now had the means to leave the city and purchase a bigger piece of the American Dream in the suburbs. White flight often meant departing the urban areas for more homogenous, mostly white enclaves in the suburbs.

**205) Big government**

The presence and influence of the federal government upon the American economy was likely largest during WWII as a follow-up to the New Deal initiatives started right after the Great Depression. "Big government" investments in the American people included the GI bill, the Veterans Administration, extensive highway funding, large-scale tax benefits for homebuyers, an astronomical surge in U.S. military defense spending, the creation of new agencies designed to better protect America with the creation of the National Security Act of 1947, along with social security programs at the federal level. The American federal government did not just spend money domestically, but it saw investment abroad as part of its plan to stay globally competitive as a viable leader and demonstrative example of the new free world. The Truman Doctrine announced March 12, 1947, which called for military aid to Greece and Turkey, the principle that the United States will contain communism wherever it threatened to expand. Additionally, the Marshall Plan announced June 5, 1947, a constituted $13 billion aid program to rebuild wartorn Europe and Japan.

# CRITICAL QUESTS

**206) Objective:** *To research the investment America made in its own economy during WWII*

Typically, business involves risk. There is no guarantee that one will be successful in business. Unless, it is wartime perhaps. Research the Wartime

Labor-Management-Government Compromise. What did it mean to have a "no-strike" pledge by labor? What did it mean for the federal government to provide "cost-plus" contracts to war manufacturers, essentially guaranteeing profits no matter what? Was this "fair" competition?

207) **Objective:** *To find the American concept of reparations*
How do the Truman Doctrine and Marshall Plan after WWII and their billion-dollar investments compare to the short-lived and failed Reconstruction period for blacks after the Civil War?

208) **Objective:** *To appreciate how underappreciated the Tuskegee Airmen remain*
*Star Wars* creator George Lucas made a contemporary movie about their experience, entitled *Redtails*, investing $65 million of his own money. The movie performed poorly at the box office. Look up comments to deduce why, despite the funding and A-list backing, the movie still performed poorly.

## CRITICAL QUESTIONS

209) **First consider:** What was the role of government in relation to American veterans of war? How was this relationship different from the one created for American veterans of enslavement?

210) **Then contemplate:** WWII fundamentally changed the world in so many ways. The United Nations was founded as an organization immediately after the war and the UN Universal Declaration on Human Rights soon followed in 1948. What did these "universal" initiatives for human rights mean for America and American blacks? What has been America's global reputation outside of the United States with respect to its human rights track record? Have you seen China's annual human rights report where they admonish America for its civil rights record?

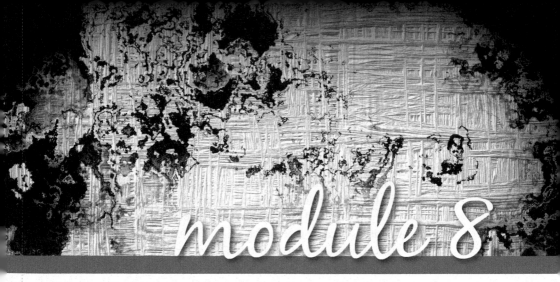

# BLACK FREEDOM MOVEMENT

*"African Americans took a significant step in raising awareness about their quest for humanity, dignity & respect."*

## PRIMARY IDEAS TO BEAR IN MIND:

A. The black freedom movement was ongoing and continuous, and predates the more well-known civil rights movement.

B. One of the key figures galvanizing the black freedom movement in the 1950s was Emmett Till, who's story still haunts us today.

C. When considering the growth of the black freedom movement in the 1950s, it is vital to recall that the "negro problem" was not limited to the South.

**A. The black freedom movement was ongoing and continuous, and predates the more well-known civil rights movement.**

## CRITICAL CONCEPTS

211) **Black Freedom Movement**

Black resistance to denied dignity has been constant and consistent since the early arrival of African slaves. After the national economy rebounded from the Great Depression and more Americans came into prosperity, more African Americans became more vocal about terminating the vestiges of Jim Crow. Black Americans went abroad to fight for freedom from 1941–1945 even though during that same period of time, Jim Crow legalized segregation was alive and well. In fact, the U.S. armed forces were not integrated until President Truman decreed for integration with Executive Order 8802 in 1948. Thus, especially after African American veterans returned from service abroad and were unable to enjoy the fruits of American democracy at home, the painful irony of Dr. W.E.B. DuBois's "twoness" of being included and excluded was too much to bear. Black Americans catapulted their cause for freedom onto a national stage with a series of carefully planned demonstrations to heighten awareness about continued black oppression.

212) *Brown v. Board of Education*

The Supreme Court decision issued in 1954 that desegregated all school systems, effectively sounding the death knell of Jim Crow legislation. The case was the result of years of strategic planning by lawyers Charles Hamilton Houston and Thurgood Marshall of the NAACP Legal Defense Fund who were able to persuasively demonstrate to Chief Justice Earl Warren and others that the fiscal disparities manifest in spending per pupil did not on its face or in principle live up to the legal fiction of "separate but equal."

213) **Southern Manifesto**

In the wake of the *Brown v. Board* decision, the Southern Manifesto was a defiant declaration signed by all but a few southern congressmen and senators that challenged the validity of the *Brown* decision, led by "Dixiecrat" leader, Gov. Strom Thurmond. The Southern Manifesto once again revived the century-long debate of states' rights versus federal enforcement of constitutional essentials.

214) **Massive Resistance**

Change is not always easy nor immediate. In the wake of the *Brown* decision, Prince Edward County in the State of Virginia decided to close ALL schools in the district rather than implement the federal mandate to integrate all schools "with all deliberate speed."

215) **Montgomery Bus Boycott**

The 1955 Montgomery Bus Boycott lasted for over a year and symbolized a rallying of a black community that finally tired of white-run corporate magnates dictating the terms of their existence. Many blacks were dependent upon the bus for transportation since many could not afford cars. Yet, in deciding not to use the Montgomery Bus System, an organic and complex system emerged enabling black workers to still make it around town. The boycott also signaled the arrival of a dynamic Baptist preacher from Georgia who became thrust into the national spotlight as a leadership force; his name was Dr. Martin Luther King, Jr.

## CRITICAL QUESTS

216) **Objective:** *To understand the relative gains of blacks*

Look up articles lauding the victory of the Montgomery Bus System. What exactly was the substance of the victory? In other words, after concluding the boycott, what could blacks point to as a tangible gain? Did blacks gain more rights and freedoms? Or did they simply fight for the privilege to pay a white company for the purpose of transportation? What would have been the political ramifications if as an outgrowth of the boycott, a self-sustaining, wholly independent means of transportation emerged for blacks in the area?

217) **Objective:** *To understand black image in the white mind*

Additionally, when we talk about the "Black Image in the White Mind," the question is how are images and narratives about humanity and superiority created and/or internalized? For more insight into this question, here are two links to two "doll tests" that speak to early identity and image formation within American society.

- *<https://www.youtube.com/watch?v=_RqsGTS5TPQ>*
- *<https://www.youtube.com/watch?v=DYCz1ppTjiM>*

How does this internalized imagery affect the public perception of black value? How would these images influence the black freedom movement?

218) **Objective:** *To understand the continuity of continued struggle*

Blacks have always struggled for freedom since they were held in captivity upon West African shores—thus, the civil rights movement did not all of a sudden begin in the 1960s. In fact, before it was a civil rights movement it was a black freedom movement. Consider what the differences may be between the two.

# CRITICAL QUESTIONS

219) **First consider:** Many people in contemporary society praise and laud the *Brown* decision as a "turning point" in American society. While certainly groundbreaking, the effects of the decision were not immediately felt. Consider how at least three state white male governors personally attempted to prevent integration of black students at public educational institutions. What does such resistance say about the roots of American racism?

220) **Then contemplate:** The Supreme Court used the vague terminology "all deliberate speed" to integrate the nation's schools. How long did it take to fully do so?

## B. One of the key figures galvanizing the black freedom movement in the 1950s was Emmett Till, who's story still haunts us today.

# CRITICAL CONCEPTS

221) **Emmett Till**
In 1955, a young African American boy of fourteen years was visiting his grandfather in Mississippi from his home city of Chicago. Confusion still exists as to what was the full nature of Till's offense. Till was downtown within a larger group and stories range from Till having said "Hey Baby" to having actually whistled at a white woman. Whatever it was, it was later communicated by the woman to her husband as "offensive" or "disrespectful." In the name of Negrophobia and having to put the negro "in his place," two men came for Emmett Till later that evening to teach him a lesson. They killed him. Brutally.

222) ***Jet* Magazine**
In the wake of the brutal murder of Emmett Till, many members of the black community were outraged that a young boy could be so coldly murdered by two men. Till's mother, despite her immeasurable grief, decided to hold an "open casket" so that "the world could done see what they did to my baby." The photo spoke for itself as Till was not recognizable except for a ring that he was wearing.

223) **Bayard Rustin**
Rustin was known as MLK's chief strategist and was also a homosexual black male. Rustin's sexual identity was largely kept secret due to concerns over rejection by the public at that time. Rustin's perspective was invaluable to King and others who erected a sustained strategy of success.

**224)** *Look* **Magazine**

The name of the magazine that purchased the story from the two white males who killed Emmett Till, J.W. Milam and Roy Bryant. The two men admitted to the killing and under the principles of "double jeopardy" were not allowed to be prosecuted twice for the same crime. They received $4,000 for their story.

**225) Jury nullification**

The principle that despite the overwhelming evidence, a jury of one's peers can still consciously make a decision in contravention of the stated law. Legal scholar Paul Butler has controversially suggested blacks consciously and deliberately use this tactic to ameliorate the disparate effects of mandatory sentencing minimums upon black males for minor drug offenses.

## CRITICAL QUESTS

**226) Objective:** *To understand the Emmett Till murder*

See if you can find photos of Emmett Till both before and after his murder. Why did his mother opt for an open casket despite the gruesome sight? Also see if you can find out who murdered Emmett and what happened to them. Lastly, for bonus, see if you can find LOCAL reaction to the murder trial and see whether or not the local community was outraged over the death of the teenage boy.

**227) Objective:** *To understand the entrenched evil of racism*

A fourteen-year-old boy senselessly lost his life. What do the (admitted) murderers do? They celebrate. They were famously seen on television emphatically kissing their wives after the "not guilty" verdict was read. See the *Eyes on Prize* documentary for this shocking footage and see what you think.

**228) Objective:** *To find out more about Strom Thurmond's history*

Meanwhile, Thurmond was pounding the pavement about the necessity to keep the races segregated and separated. Also, Thurmond wished to keep separate information and news about how he fathered a child out of wedlock with a woman not his wife—an African American woman. How do you think Thurmond in his mind reconciled the tensions between fear and fascination of black images?

© Joseph Sohm/Shutterstock.com

## CRITICAL QUESTIONS

**229)** **First consider:** When did the Emmett Till murder take place? Only one year after *Brown v Board*. What does the Till murder suggest about the rate of change in the postwar society?

**230)** **Then contemplate:** "All deliberate speed" was vague. While some states sought to implement the *Brown* decision, others like Mississippi still reported no blacks attending schools with whites in the year 1964. Is the problem at least solved for today?

## C. When considering the growth of the black freedom movement in the 1950s, it is vital to recall that the "negro problem" was not limited to the South.

## CRITICAL CONCEPTS

**231)** **White Citizens' Councils**
White Citizen's Councils were the suburbs' answer to what the "band of brothers" sought to create in the aftermath of the Civil War. Although nowhere as brash and overt as the KKK, they were seen as much more genteel, organized, and refined. Yet, many of the aims were the same. Under the auspices of expressing "concern" over neighborhood safety, such councils sought to limit or eliminate black presence within their neighborhoods. These councils claimed 250,000 members by 1956.

**232)** **"The Great Pretender"**
"The Great Pretender" was the first song by a black act to reach the top (#1) of the Pop (white) charts in the United States in November 1955. It

also went to the #1 spot on the U.S. R&B charts and #5 in the U.K. Rock-n-Roll started off as quite diverse and brought together equally diverse audiences to hear this new pulse of vibrant, energetic music.

**233) George Wallace**

Democratic Alabama governor who at his inaugural address promised "Segregation now, segregation tomorrow, segregation forever!" to deafening crowd cheers. Wallace attempted to block school integration in 1963 and gave his blessing to police chief Bull O'Connor to have fire hoses turned on demonstrators in Birmingham, 1963.

**234) Rebel culture**

In the 1950s, while the black freedom movement was frowned upon or ignored altogether, many impulses and strands of rebellion were manifest in mainstream culture:

- Movie icons of rebellion: James Dean, Marlon Brando
- Literature of youthful rebellion:
  J.D. Salinger, *A Catcher in the Rye* (1951)
  Allen Gisberg, "Howl" (1955)
  Jack Kerouac, *On the Road* (1957)
  Norman Mailer, "The White Negro" (1957)
- Kinsey's *Sexual Behavior in the Human Male* (1948) and *Sexual Behavior in the Human Female* (1953). Both argue that premarital sex, marital infidelity, homosexuality are more prevalent than assumed.

Yet, when blacks "rebelled" against romantic racialist notions of "know your place," and chose to vociferously fight for fundamental constitutional rights, that was viewed as a problem.

**235) Joseph McCarthy**

A senator from Wisconsin who staked his career on red baiting, or on finding and rooting out rogue communists within America. McCarthy's public antics helped contribute toward the Red Scare, where anyone associated with communists or communist philosophies were not to be trusted. Many Jews and blacks came under scrutiny for their political beliefs. McCarthy never found anyone guilty of lying about their communist ties; he died shortly after leaving office from alcoholism.

## CRITICAL QUESTS

**236) Objective:** *To research how manifest the black image in the white mind was*

When considering the growth of the black freedom movement in the 1950s, let us recall that the "negro problem" was not limited to the South.

Observe this link and note what part of the country it is coming from (*<http://depts.washington.edu/civilr/coon_chicken.htm>*). What do the authors state was the ultimate reason for why the establishment closed?

237) **Objective: *To find what made homogeneity so popular***

Irving Howe's essay "Age of Conformity" (1953) characterizes American culture as increasingly homogeneous, marginalizing dissent, and conflict. Do you find conformity to be as prevalent today? Is it higher among residents in the inner city or in the suburbs?

238) **Objective: *To appreciate growth of suburbia***

With the steady growth of the gross national product from 1950–1985, auto sales also went up tremendously from 1940–1970. Thus, in 1945 there were only 8 shopping centers in the United States, but by 1950 there were almost 4,000. Look up early suburban racially restrictive covenants and consider this: How did such rapid growth slow racial integration?

© Everett Historical/Shutterstock.com

## CRITICAL QUESTIONS

239) **First consider:** What did the House Un-American Activities Committee accomplish aside from generating apprehension and anxiety?

240) **Then contemplate:** *Brown v. Board II* was a second Supreme Court decision required to clarify the meaning of "all deliberate speed" given the manifold issues in implementation across the country. Find Dr. W.E.B. DuBois's 1957 article on the topic and decide whether you agree or disagree with his stance?

*Introduction to African-American Studies*

# CIVIL RIGHTS MOVEMENT

*"The initial quest by African Americans was broadened into an initiative that secured more protections for all Americans, including African Americans."*

## PRIMARY IDEAS TO BEAR IN MIND:

A. The civil rights movement is an extension and broadening of the black freedom movement—in other words, what started off as exclusive to blacks opened up to appeal to a broader audience.

B. A key piece of legislation that emerged from the civil rights movement was the 1964 Civil Rights Act.

C. The 1965 Voting Rights Act was likely the second most important piece of legislation to emerge during this period.

**A. The civil rights movement is an extension and broadening of the black freedom movement—in other words, what started off as exclusive to blacks opened up to appeal to a broader audience.**

## CRITICAL CONCEPTS

241) **Civil Rights Movement**

The civil rights movement is an extension and broadening of the black freedom movement—in other words, what started off as exclusive to blacks opened up to appeal to a broader audience. While blacks remain at the center of most images associated with this movement, consider how successful such a movement would have been if it had remained "a black thing," and did not receive the support of antiwar, gay rights, student and women's rights protesters as well. It is common knowledge that all of the protest groups mentioned in the previous sentence "borrowed" freely from successful techniques and slogans used by blacks; many a court case for other protest groups makes analogies to blacks and their legalized marginalization as the ultimate metaphor that other sectors of society should also avoid.

242) **Pettus Bridge**

Otherwise known as "Bloody Sunday," a fateful day when on March 7, 1965, Alabama state police attacked peaceful, unarmed marchers crossing Pettus Bridge as part of a larger voting rights drive. Despite the passage of the Civil Rights Act in 1964, racial tensions about the "rightful place" of blacks in society were nonetheless high. The calamity was captured on video and broadcast on television for all to see, now casting a new light upon the effect of media, thereby generating additional public sympathy for the civil rights movement.

243) **Freedom Riders**

In 1961, a group of individuals who fearlessly rode buses from the North into the Deep South to heighten awareness and register blacks to vote as a means to lawfully work within the system to peacefully advocate for desired change. The bitter irony is that despite taking every precaution to engage the political process properly, they were the victim of vigilante, terroristic attacks on May 4, 1961. Buses were bombed, and riders attempting to escape were dragged from the wreckage and savagely beaten in full view of police in Rock Hill, South Carolina. The riders vowed to continue, and on May 20 arrived in Montgomery to a mob of 1,000 and no police. Riders were knocked unconscious, at least all riders hospitalized. Finally, the riders were arrested in Jackson, Mississippi, upon arrival and 300 Freedom Riders served time in Mississippi prisons. Since several of the volunteers were white liberal college students from the North, the Freedom Riders phenomena connected both the North and South.

244) *The Other America*

*The Other America*, a book by Michael Harrington (1962), exposed how the postwar boom was primarily reserved for Americans of a particular race: white. During Kennedy's reign when the book was written, blacks suffered more so than whites in virtually every statistical metric. Kennedy did not initially do much to alleviate racial tensions as he equivocated upon civil rights despite having a good reputation for addressing the issues. On Kennedy's watch were numerous public housing desegregation delays in addition to an ineffectual record for the President's Committee on Equal Employment.

245) **Student Non-Violent Coordinating Committee**

The SNCC formed in 1960 and coordinated a wave of sit-in protests, which emerged as a powerful nonviolent tool of resistance. Participants in sit-ins had to undergo training and screening since suppressing the natural instinct to defend oneself could be maliciously interpreted as an act of violence that would undercut the strategy of exposing white vitriol for commonsense integration within society. SNCC observed a decentralized leadership and a participatory democracy as opposed to the more conservative Southern Christian Leadership Conference. SNCC adhered to nonviolence, BUT acknowledged the possible need for increased militancy and confrontation.

# CRITICAL QUESTS

246) **Objective:** *To understand the influence of media*

Look up images concerning the training for the lunch counter sit-in scene in the 2013 movie *The Butler*. What happens if these images are not seen by an international audience? How does interest convergence play a role? Look up authentic footage online to see how much corresponds with the scene from the movie *The Butler*. Who appears to be behaving poorly in these videos?

247) **Objective:** *To understand the power of image*

In the essay by Norman Mailer, "Superman Comes to the Supermarket" (1960), Mailer argues that media played a significant role in framing

Kennedy as an "everyday man" who would appeal to the masses for presidential votes. While positioned as a liberal, look up Kennedy's actual civil rights record, from 1960–1962. Kennedy promised to make civil rights a priority during the 1960 election; he named a presidential committee to look into employment discrimination in federal contracts. The committee accomplished little. After promising to desegregate federally funded housing projects, Kennedy refused to act until 1962 and refused to take a stand supporting a civil rights act. To what degree is Kennedy's presidency similar to Lincoln's with respect to enjoying a positive reputation despite being ambivalent about race.

248) **Objective:** *To understand the impact of the black freedom movement*
Based upon the discussion of the black freedom movement's morphing into the larger and broader civil rights movement, reflect upon how your life might be different today if there was no black freedom struggle when you think of your civil rights.

# CRITICAL QUESTIONS

249) **First consider:** In assessing the civil rights movement, did blacks gain equality? Or equal rights?

250) **Then contemplate:** When did "Bloody Sunday" occur? Two years after the March on Washington (e.g., "I Have a Dream" speech) and one year after the signing of the 1964 Civil Rights Act. Why then would racial tensions be so high despite such groundbreaking progress?

## B. A key piece of legislation that emerged from the civil rights movement was the 1964 Civil Rights Act.

# CRITICAL CONCEPTS

251) **1964 Civil Rights Act**
One of 1964 act's key features was the protection of rights in the workplace with the creation of the Equal Employment Opportunity Commission (EEOC). What may seem basic, logical, or commonplace now—the idea that one should not be subject to racial discrimination whether they work for a private or public employer was new and revolutionary at the time. Private businesses until that time "had the right" to discriminate. A

delicate line still exists over private employers choosing whomever they want to work for them versus mistreating people and refusing to work with them just because of their race—the latter still being so very abstract and difficult to detect, let alone enforce. The 1964 Civil Rights Act applies to every American, regardless of race, creed, religion, or gender. While originally written for blacks, other protected classes (such as women) were added to the bill at the last minute as a possible attempt to sink it by dissuading congressional voters who might have believed that such a measure was going too "over the top." Three major outcomes are that Title VII banned segregation and discrimination:

- in all public accommodations;
- within employment on the basis of race, ethnicity, religion, or sex; and
- created the Equal Employment Opportunity Commission to police employment bias.

**252) James Baldwin**

Baldwin is one of America's most gifted writers; it is shameful that so few students know about this national treasure. In this short but powerful librette, Baldwin powerfully articulates the complex feelings of African Americans who still battle the "twoness" or double consciousness of being both included yet excluded by American mainstream society simultaneously. Such a balancing act requires vast amounts of mental and spiritual energy, yet Baldwin offers an innovative prescription to his nephew in "The Fire Next Time."

© Vector FX/Shutterstock.com

**253) Ross Barnett**

The third governor using state power to contravene the Supreme Court's ruling in *Brown v. Board* in a stand-off entitled "Ole Miss Crisis" (1962). Black male James Meredith enrolled at the University of Mississippi, but Gov. Barnett (D-MS) attempted to block his enrollment. Kennedy ordered in U.S. marshals and National Guard troops to Oxford, Mississippi, to protect Meredith; a riot ensued.

**254) Democratic governors**

At least three Democratic governors attempted to prevent integration within their state in defiance of federal incursion upon states' rights:

- Gov. Orval Faubus (D-AR) tried to preserve segregation; Pres. Eisenhower intervened by calling in the 101st Airborne in Little Rock, 1957.
- Gov. George Wallace (D-AL) personally blocked the entrance to integrated school registration.
- Gov. Ross Barnett personally blocks the University of Mississippi in 1962 to prevent James Meredith from registering; President Kennedy intervened by calling in the National Guard.

**255) Letter from a Birmingham Jail**

Composed on Good Friday, April 12, 1963, this writing was an elegant, yet acerbic critique of the white southern clergy who opposed King and his tactics when King's position was that his cause for constitutional rights was a righteous one. King's appeal was not wholly effective as merely two months later, activist Medgar Evers was assassinated June 12, 1963.

# CRITICAL QUESTS

**256) Objective:** *To understand how many times America has tried to "get it right"*

Look up how many civil rights acts have been passed in the history of our country. Are you surprised?

**257) Objective:** *To understand black emotion*

Look up the poet and poems of Ether Popel, "Blasphemy—American Style" and "Flag Salute." How does Popel choose to communicate her sentiments? What are her sentiments?

**258) Objective:** *To find the genius in Baldwin*

Look up the following link, take note, and then take notes: <*https://www. youtube.com/watch?v=L0L5fciA6AU*>

# CRITICAL QUESTIONS

259) **First consider:** Was President Kennedy effective for civil rights or not? Was he as ambivalent as Lincoln or not? Before Kennedy was assassinated, he pledged support for passage of a Civil Rights Act, June 1963; authorized development of an anti-poverty initiative; pledged support for passage of a Civil Rights Act, June 1963; and authorized development of an antipoverty initiative. Did Lyndon B. Johnson shamelessly exploit this momentum with campaign slogans exhorting "let us continue"? Or, was the "Johnson treatment" necessary to push the civil rights agenda in ways that Kennedy would not?

260) **Then contemplate:** What would society look like if a legal case for *Brown v. Board* was not made? See Derrick Bell, *Har L Rev* 93:518 (1980).

## C. The 1965 Voting Rights Act was likely the second most important piece of legislation to emerge during this period.

# CRITICAL CONCEPTS

261) **1965 Voting Rights Act**
This act was likely the second most important piece of legislation to emerge during this period. It did not grant blacks the right to vote, for the Fifteenth Amendment spoke to that issue. It was designed to keep mostly southern states honest as scores of infractions were still being reported about blacks in the South having their right to vote abridged by local authorities. Johnson responded by endorsing the Voting Rights Act, signed August 6, 1965. Addressing Congress, he says "We shall overcome."

262) **Moynihan Report**
This report is key because of how it changed the landscape of public debate over how to fix the "negro problem," and more importantly, who was responsible for the ails of black folk stuck and trapped in the ghetto. In essence, Senator Patrick Moynihan identified black males in particular and inherently dysfunctional family dynamics generally as the roots of the problem in America.[1]

263) **Freedom Summer**
The impact of the Mississippi "Freedom Summer" was that in 1964, civil rights organizations SNCC, CORE, and NAACP joined in an effort to target Mississippi with voter registration, "Freedom Schools," and the

formation of a political party (the Mississippi Freedom Democratic Party) to challenge the state's segregationist mainline Democratic Party.

**264) Hot Summers**

Race riots broke out all over the country as a result of mounting tensions in densely populated urban areas where black citizens voiced anger and concern over heavy-handed police tactics. Such tensions began to boil over at the beginning of more strident rhetoric espoused from black leaders such as Stokely Carmichael and Malcolm X, whose autobiography in 1998 was voted by *Time* magazine as one of the ten most influential nonfiction books of the twentieth century. Malcolm was assassinated February 21, 1965.

**265) Office of Economic Opportunity Act**

The OEO Act was launched in 1964 as part of President Johnson's "Great Society," or his attempt to continue investing within the American public as a means to safeguard its future. Johnson launched a "War on Poverty," allocating $1 billion to antipoverty programs; however, unlike the New Deal following the Great Depression, most of the targeted recipients of the OEO's investment dollars were nonwhite citizens.

## CRITICAL QUESTS

**266) Objective: *To research continuing confusion about rights***

When the twenty-seven-year oversight period stipulated in the 1965 Voting Rights Act ended in 1992, there was much consternation over whether blacks would lose their right to vote. Look up articles from 1992 and determine why there would still be mass confusion over blacks having or exercising their right to vote.

**267) Objective: *To find out more of the black image in the white mind***

Look up the "Moynihan Report," Ch. III "The Roots of the Problem," U.S. Department of Labor, March 1965, and see whether you agree with Moynihan's rationale or whether he makes that which has been historically racist (i.e., romantic racialism, temininity and Negrophobia) sound and appear more reasonable and rational.

**268) Objective: *To appreciate the influence of media***

The 1960 Kennedy-Nixon televised debate is largely credited with providing Kennedy the presidential election victory. Kennedy came off smooth and polished in contrast to a flustered, sweaty Nixon. See if you can find original footage online. To what extent did Kennedy's positive media portrayal influence public opinion? What does this incident say about the growing power of media in mainstream society?

## CRITICAL QUESTIONS

269) **First consider:** How much of America was directly inspired by the black freedom movement and its tactics that became public and popularized in the 1950s?
- Student protests begin in Berkeley and San Francisco, May 1960
- National Organization of Women founded in 1966 by Betty Friedan (R), Dr. Kathryn Clarenbach, and others, which promoted equal rights for women and engaged in consciousness raising by protesting "Miss America," 1968
- Columbia University student protestors, 1968
- American Indian Movement, founded 1968
- Gay rights movement Stonewall Riot (1969), which constituted a confrontation in Greenwich Village, NYC, which marked the emergence of a militant gay rights movement
- Weatherman's "Days of Rage" Chicago, 1969
- La Raza Unida founded, 1969 as an outgrowth of burgeoning Chicano rights movement, which featured Cesar Chavez of the United Farm Workers Union
- Occupation of Alcatraz Island, San Francisco Bay, 1969
- Vietnam veterans against the war, 1972
- AIM occupies Bureau of Indian Affairs in Washington, 1972
- Wounded Knee, South Dakota, occupation and standoff, 1973

270) **Then contemplate:** How much of the civil rights movement was characterized by violence? Violence by who? Violence for what justifiable reason?

## Footnotes:

[1] The "Moynihan Report" was composed by Senator Daniel Patrick Moynihan in 1965. "The Negro Family: The Case for National Action." *Office of Policy Planning and Research.* United States Department of Labor. March, 1965.

# module 10

# VIETNAM AND BLACK RADICALISM

---

*"The sour distaste of war also soured the outlook of many African Americans still longsuffering for equality; more pointed critiques emerged as a result."*

---

## PRIMARY IDEAS TO BEAR IN MIND:

A. The Vietnam war was a very fractious period in American history that still strikes as a contentious issue.

B. Black radicalism quite frankly gets a bad rap.

C. Black radicalism's biggest threat may not have been in changing the system, but its attempt to create new ones.

## A. The Vietnam war was a very fractious period in American history that still strikes as a contentious issue.

## CRITICAL CONCEPTS

**271) Vietnam War**

Unlike the 1940s where war was celebrated as a means to flex global might, collective consensus on the Vietnam war was more divided. Many were confused over the U.S. role in the war and many in the public were at odds over the ultimate end goal.

© Keith Terrier/Shutterstock.com

## 272) Cu Chi Tunnels

As evidence of a worthy opponent, these intricate systems of tunnels demonstrated that the United States and all of its military might could nonetheless be humbled and brought down to size. Viet Cong soldiers crafted small tunnels as part of a larger guerilla warfare strategy that kept many American troops guessing and on edge.

© View Apart/Shutterstock.com

© chiakto/Shutterstock.com

273) **"Re-tired Sandals"**

As additional evidence of the resourcefulness and resilience of the Viet Cong, soldiers and their supporters were forethinkers in "sustainability," having recycled many American bombs that did not detonate or in having acquired old, used tires and making sandals out of them.

274) **"19"**

The average age of the infantryman killed in the line of duty. Many of those who were on the frontlines were African American.

275) **Body Count**

On the nightly news, Americans were shown raw footage of the Vietnam theater on their home televisions. News stations kept a rolling tally of American soldiers who perished in the line of duty. The body count number became a symbolic focal point of everything contentious with the Vietnam war.

## CRITICAL QUESTS

276) **Objective: *To understand how tumultuous the 1970s were***

Look up and listen to the link to Marvin Gaye's genius album, "What's Going On?": *<http://www.youtube.com/watch?v=7vXCGscrVeE>*

Listen to the first 20:06 which comprise the following six tracks; see if you can determine when one song ends and the next one begins:

01 "What's Going On"
02 "What's Happening Brother"
03 "Flyin' High (In the Friendly Sky)"
04 "Save the Children"
05 "God Is Love"
06 "Mercy Mercy Me (The Ecology)"

277) **Objective:** *To understand the "shame" of Vietnam*

While many oppose our current military activity abroad, not nearly as many Americans are as vocal and as visible about it. This might be due to the amount of information we have circulating within our mainstream media. Many Americans currently may waffle if asked who we are fighting, where, and for how long. Perhaps, it is because we have so many other options for news and information, whether it be OMG! reports, Jon Stewart, or Fox News. Back then (ask your parents), there were fewer channels so there was more of a shared consciousness about the same information. For example, anyone you know over the age of sixty remembers this influential report vividly: *<http://www.youtube.com/watch?v=S3mfXnFtwQc>*

278) **Objective:** *To understand why America was in Vietnam in the first place*

Look up the entry date for U.S. involvement in Vietnam. Is the date as celebrated as December 7, 1941? Was the rationale for entering clear from the beginning?

# CRITICAL QUESTIONS

279) **First consider:** King publicly opposes the war in Vietnam in April 1967. What do you think this opposition did for his image? Why was it not discussed more often?

280) **Then contemplate:** What did a renewed emphasis on law and order mean for blacks within inner cities? For whites within the suburbs?

## B. Black radicalism quite frankly gets a bad rap.

# CRITICAL CONCEPTS

**281) Franz Fanon**

Fanon lived a relatively short life from 1925 to 1961, but made a large philosophical impact upon oppressed and marginalized groups of people globally. Martinique-born, he was a psychiatrist stationed in Algeria during the Algerian uprising against France, which began in 1954. He became radicalized and became most famous for Peau Noire, Masques Blancs (1952) [Black Skin, White Masks (translated, 1967)] and Damnes de la Terre (1961) [The Wretched of the Earth (translated 1965)]—works that became widely circulated as many African and Caribbean nations sought their political independence during the early 1960s.

**282) King, 2.0**

King later in his life began moving toward an economic based agenda rather than a civil rights agenda. King took his movement northward to Chicago and other cities, facilitating protest marches in and around Chicago in 1966, placing King in conflict with Mayor Richard Daley. King was then blamed by Daley for a race riot that occurred in Chicago, 1966 as reflective of more scrutiny placed upon King as he organized a Poor People's Campaign from 1967–1968. In fact, King was helping organize in Memphis, Tennessee, a sanitation workers strike before he was assassinated April 4, 1968.

**283) Affirmative Action**

The beginnings of Affirmative Action were set in motion by the Philadelphia Plan, which in 1969 set racial quotas and timetables in hiring by federal contractors.

Plumbers in Philadelphia in 1969:

| | |
|---|---|
| total: | 2,335 |
| white: | 2,322 |
| black: | 12 |

Yet, strident academic rhetoric effectively dissuaded the public from accepting such a plan as for the "greater good." Nathan Glazer in "The Limits of Social Policy," Commentary 52 (September 1971): 51-58 argued that government social policies are less effective in solving social problems than liberals have hoped. Thus, policy makers operate with imperfect knowledge of social forces and in attempting to solve problems, unintended consequences are created. Glazer suggested that private market solutions might be more effective than public policy in solving social problems thereby obviating any need for the government to become active in balancing an economy that will achieve balance on its own.

284) *Newsweek* **Magazine**

A *Newsweek* poll in 1969 showed that a plurality of Americans believed that blacks had a better chance than white of getting a good job, a decent house, and adequate schooling. This poll is not dispositive, yet demonstrative of a stubborn reluctance by whites to share in the fruits of American democracy. This poll rather reveals a mindset consistent with "zero-sum game theory," whereby many whites reflexively felt that "more rights" (or restored or recognized rights, rather) for blacks meant "less rights" for whites. Nixon effectively spoke to this victimhood with the silent majority strategy.

285) **Stagflation**

With the gas crisis of 1973–1974, the American economy also experienced "The Great Inflation," or the biggest wave of inflation in the twentieth century triggered in large part by rising energy prices. A 1973-74 Embargo by the Organization of Petroleum Exporting Countries (OPEC) against the United States for its support of Israel during the "Yom Kippur War" of 1973 contributed greatly toward "Stagflation," or the phenomena when inflation and unemployment rise simultaneously. This economic downturn increased pressure to create dual income families for all Americans, with such pressure exacerbated for black workers experiencing difficulty finding gainful employment in the first place. During this time period, married women with children increasingly enter the workforce but fewer jobs are available unlike the boom experienced immediately after WWII ended. America's once-strong auto industry suffered major losses of high waged manufacturing jobs and auto, steel, and other industries announced massive layoffs and plant closings, with many of the jobs lost being unionized, high-wage jobs. Black security with the marketplace was even more precarious.

## CRITICAL QUESTS

286) **Objective:** *To understand black militants*

Let's think logically: what were blacks militant about? What were they speaking out against? We must be very careful not to dismiss groups like the Black Panthers and individual orators like Malcolm X as anti-American when ironically they were vociferously advocating for a better America. To want the government and its citizens to live up to its constitutional obligation is highly rational. But recall what Fredrickson said about Negrophobia (negro as beast) and how it affects the black image in the white mind. Blacks who appear frustrated about being oppressed and mistreated are now nothing more than "angry" dissidents who must be shut down and shut up (<*http://ia341313.us.archive.org/1/items/Malcolm_X/Malcolm_X_House_Negro_and_Field_Negro.mp3*>).

Feel free to listen again to Malcolm X (<*https://www.youtube.com/watch?v=gRSgUTWffMQ*>) and decide for yourself whether he makes a persuasive case toward the end of this clip, that if violence is used against an individual, then perhaps that individual can at least signal that he or she is prepared to use violence to prevent a repeat violent attack. In other words, is Malcolm promoting irrational racist rhetoric? Or is it a rational response to repeated and rampant race-based repression?

287) **Objective:** *To understand white radicalism*
Barry Goldwater once claimed that "extremism in the defense of liberty is no vice." Otherwise known as the father of the "law and order" phrase, Goldwater conveniently ignored the raw economic and racial disorder precipitating such crime-heavy conditions within the inner city. Goldwater's rhetoric laid the groundwork for "new Jim Crow" policies based upon a more nuanced Negrophobia that positioned whites as the "victims" of an overbearing welfare funding government that did too little to protect honest citizens who actually worked for their just share.

288) **Objective:** *To understand the violent reputation of black radicals*
For those feeling feisty, reflect instead on WHY the Black Panthers/Malcolm X are considered violent and militant? Again, if we agree that the KKK was/is an example of violence, consider in turn, how many crosses did the Black Panthers burn? How many white churches did the Black Panthers bomb? How many whites did the Black Panthers lynch? Find out what you can through research.

# CRITICAL QUESTIONS

289) **First consider:** There is a long history of black radicalism stretching back to the early arrival of African slaves. Some such moments in time include:
   - Plantation resistance
   - Underground Railroad
   - Abolitionists
   - Civil War veterans

- Garveyites
- Double V supporters
- Black freedom movement
- Civil rights movement
- Black power movement

Why are individuals like Malcolm X and groups like the Black Panthers considered radical if they merely are the latest strand of a long, continuous strand of resistance? How is Malcolm X any more radical than Frederick Douglass? Speaking of radical, how do African American historical actors fighting for freedom stack up against other American patriots such as Patrick Henry who once famously said, "Give me liberty or give me death"? How different is Malcolm X's message of "By any means necessary," especially if we insert the word "liberty" at the beginning of X's phrase? Is X then also an American patriot?

290) **Then contemplate:** With the Supreme Court *Griggs v. Duke Power* decision in 1971, the Court found that it was not necessary to prove intent to discriminate as consistent patterns of discriminatory results required affirmative remedies. Historian Nancy MacLean writes that "resurgent corporate political power brought renewed popular white support for private property rights over human rights." Thus, by the 1970s, many whites were fatigued and were no longer interested in collective human rights (for blacks). What does this development mean for blacks who "gained" civil rights less than a decade earlier? What does this development mean for the Civil Rights Act?

**B. Black radicalism's biggest threat may not have been in changing the system, but its attempt to create new ones.**

# CRITICAL CONCEPTS

291) **"Tricky Dick"**

President Richard Nixon was controversial for several reasons, the Watergate scandal notwithstanding. Yet, Nixon also was recorded saying the word "jigaboo" as contemporary presidents have their phone conversations recorded [www.alternet.org/story/17422]. What does this one word signify for black Americans still looking for a shot for the American Dream? Silent Majority. With a renewed emphasis on southern voters, Nixon was able to help Republicans reclaim the White House. In 1968, Nixon had won only 38% of the southern vote. In 1972, he won 70%. In 1968, Nixon had won only 35%

of the blue-collar vote. By 1972, he won 54% of this vote. To this extent, Kevin Phillips, in *The Emerging Republican Majority* (1969), argued that the 1968 election portends a realignment in American politics whereby an emerging republican majority would capitalize on two primary sectors:

- Growth of the South and Southwest "Sunbelt"
- Growth of Suburbia

292) **Nation of Islam**

Considered a radical offshoot from traditional Islam, it was framed as a black man's religion free from psychological poisoning of Christianity. The group was conservative and emphasized meticulous external and formal appearance, strict observation of gender lines, and respect for fellow members of the community. The nation's leader, the Honorable Elijah Muhammad, selected Malcolm X to be its most visible spokesperson.

293) **"Southern Strategy"**

A controversial political strategy to appeal to those who harbored deep-seated, latent racial discontent, but were shamed from expressing themselves truthfully and publicly due to recent civil rights "gains." The Southern Strategy was multifaceted, and included increased investments within law enforcement to "take back the streets" as part of the law and order campaign. Also Nixon had two failed Supreme Court nominees who were partial to southern racial politics in Clement Haynesworth (R-SC) and Harold Carswell (R-FL) Nixon also met with Sen. Strom Thurmond, June 1, 1968, where Thurmond supported Nixon and exacted promises from him regarding the protection of southern interests related to civil rights. Finally Nixon cut back on Lyndon B. Johnson's Great Society and the OEO was eliminated by 1973.

294) **Black Panthers**

The Black Panthers are widely referred to as a radical organization. The group was founded in 1966 in Oakland, California, by Huey Newton and Bobby Seale. While known for wearing all black and exercising their Second Amendment rights, several additional features of the organization include:

- A self-defense focus
- A hot breakfast program
- Armed citizens patrols
- 10,000 members @ peak in 1969
- Drug and alcohol rehab
- Medical clinics
- Classes on politics and economics
- Clothing distribution
- Prison transportation

© Mr. Interior/Shutterstock.com

**295) Tommie Smith and John Carlos**

At the Mexico City Summer Olympics of 1968, these two track and field medal winners used the medal platform as a larger political platform to make a protest against brutality against blacks in the United States. The protest consisted of Smith and Carlos splitting a pair of black gloves with one wearing the left hand and one wearing the right hand. They both stuck their gloved hands in the air with their hands forming fists and their heads down while the national anthem played. Smith and Carlos paid the price of social ostracization upon their return to the states.

## CRITICAL QUESTS

**296) Objective:** *To research and listen*

Malcolm X's "House Negro vs. Field Negro" speech contains a well-known metaphor and speech delivered from one considered "militant" during his time. But let us bring logic back into the equation. As much as we all agree and stated that if we were Anne Moody or worse enslaved, we would not like it, etc., what then do we think of Malcolm's statement that as a field negro he would pray for wind. Does this mean that Malcolm is filled with hate? For him to wish an end to his suffering and oppression that was fostered by the hate of another at no fault of his own?

297) **Objective:** *To appreciate true radicalism*

Listen and/or read James Baldwin's rhetoric very carefully ["Baldwin's N*gger" <*https://youtu.be/ryuAW_gnjYQ*>]. Who's rhetoric is more fiery? Baldwin or X's?

298) **Objective:** *To learn the high price of high morals*

In looking up this video link about the Black Power Salute, consider whether you think the action is crazed, angry, and irrational or the opposite (<*http://www.youtube.com/watch?v=NAaacHuPgTE*>). Also in considering extremism and how MLK, Medgar Evers, Malcolm X, and James Meredith have all been fired upon, how many political white actors have been shot by blacks?

## CRITICAL QUESTIONS

299) **First consider:** Jesse Helms received political support from the KKK in 1970s. Why or how can the KKK be politically relevant over 100 years after its founding?

300) **Then contemplate:** The famous Kerner Report stated that white society is deeply implicated in the ghetto. White institutions created it, white institutions maintain it, and white society condones it. Do you agree or disagree? Why or why not?

# REAGANOMICS

*"After decades of federal social programming, the government was now seen as the problem; Reagan's 'small government' and 'War on Drugs' policies significantly impacted African Americans accordingly."*

## PRIMARY IDEAS TO BEAR IN MIND:

A. After years of dominant Democratic rule, Reagan's presidency marked the triumphant return of Republicans, conservatism, and fiscal control to the White House.

B. Unfortunately, a return of conservatism also brought a return of Negrophobia.

C. The "War on Drugs" based upon its execution, could be appropriately retitled, "War on (black) Thugs."

A. After years of dominant Democratic rule, Reagan's presidency marked the triumphant return of Republicans, conservatism, and fiscal control to the White House.

## CRITICAL CONCEPTS

**301) Gerald Ford Era**

A rather nondescript era in American history or politics; Ford took over after Nixon was impeached and resigned from office in 1974. Ford served only less than three years but bears the distinction as the first and only nonelected president of the United States.

**302) Jimmy Carter Era**

Elected into office in 1976, the Carter campaign represented the return of Democratic rule to the White House after the Nixon era. Carter positioned himself as a populist choice, hailing upon his "Georgia peanut farmer" roots. Carter actually walked Pennsylvania Avenue on his way to the White House after his inauguration on the Capitol steps to symbolize that he was "one of the people." Carter likely follows Ford with respect to presidencies with little to report.

**303) Hard Hat demonstrations**

Mayor John Lindsay of New York City lowered the flag to half mast at city hall to mourn the death of the Kent State students shot dead by law enforcement on their own campus. Construction workers in Lower Manhattan marched on city hall, raised the flag back to full staff, and beat up antiwar protestors along the way. This demonstration reflected the rise of the white ethnic and the widely shared belief that white males were in actuality being left out of the picture when the nation spent time obsessing about the rights and welfare of others.

**304) Reaganomics**

Reagan's presidency marked the return of Republicans and conservatism to the White House. Before, the government had been characterized by its social programs

© Joseph Sohm/Shutterstock.com

*Introduction to African-American Studies*

designed to help the public with the New Deal after the Depression, the Fair Deal, and the Great Society in the 1960s—now the government and all of its largess was now the problem and these social programs came under attack. The emphasis on "small government" became prominent now that a bloated, invasive, and inefficient federal government was seen as the problem.

**305) Star Wars**

In honor of a widely popular movie series by the same name that debuted in the late 1970s, the "Star Wars" missile defense program was a cold war initiative where in the event Russia would send nuclear warheads toward the United States, a combination of satellite technology in space and weaponry on the ground and sea would allow for rapid defense and response, theoretically enabling for the destruction of such a warhead while it was in the air. This initiative cost billions of dollars but was considered a sound investment in the country's security in contrast to social programs that were seen as unnecessary and bleeding the coffers dry.

## CRITICAL QUESTS

**306) Objective:** *To understand how much defense spending increased*
Look up the differences in defense spending from the Carter years to the Reagan era. Was the threat of nuclear war a real justification for such spending?

**307) Objective:** *To understand how much social programming decreased*
Look up the differences in social spending from the Johnson years to the Reagan era. Why the departure from the past pattern of investing in the American people?

**308) Objective:** *To understand Reagan's change of position, from union president to union buster*
Reagan forcefully broke the PATCO strike by directly challenging the power of labor unions. Reagan delivered an ultimatum for striking workers to comply, and promptly fired everyone after the deadline, installing the National Guard to continue operation of air traffic control towers so that planes could fly and that the economy could continue unhindered. Reagan's bold tactics inspired other employers to replace strikers. Reagan also appointed union opponents to the National Labor Relations Board. The irony of Reagan's later position against organized labor is that he

started off his career as president of the Screen Actors Guild, one of the more established, historical examples of organized labor that the country has ever known.

## CRITICAL QUESTIONS

309) **First consider:** How did whites come to see themselves as victims of a bloated federal government just two generations removed from Depression-era New Deal programming, WWII "cost-plus" contracts, and increased cold war defense spending?

310) **Then contemplate:** How did popular television shows such as *All in the Family* (featuring television character Archie Bunker, 1971–1979) or movies such as *Joe* help to spread negative propaganda about white fright?

## B. Unfortunately, a return of conservatism also brought a return of Negrophobia.

## CRITICAL CONCEPTS

311) **Welfare Queen**

The term "Welfare Queen" became popularized during Reagan's 1976 failed presidential campaign. The Welfare Queen was the horrific image that combined many historical narratives into one body: an overweight, heavy set, dark-skinned black female that had multiple kids with no father figure(s) in sight, sitting on her couch all the day long watching television with a cereal bowl in her lap while waiting for her next government assistance check to arrive via mail.

Much conservative popular literature supported this view: George Gilder, in *Wealth and Poverty* (1980), argued that welfare is cruel because it helps to create "dependency." Charles Murray in *Losing Ground* (1984) argued that efforts to create American social policies for the poor have hurt the poor more than helped them. Fredrickson, in *Black Image of the White Mind*, argued that whites projected onto blacks images of unchecked sexuality and laziness as researched and substantiated by Martin Gilens (2000). "The News Media and the Racialization of Poverty." *Why Americans Hate Welfare: Race, Media, and the Politics of Antipoverty Pol-*

*Introduction to African-American Studies*

*icy.* Studies in Communication, Media, and Public Opinion. Chicago, IL: University of Chicago Press. pp. 102–32.

The Welfare Queen thus symbolized a social policy crisis was deemed to be at hand since efforts to reform welfare under Nixon and Carter were largely seen as unsuccessful.

## 312) Boston Busing Crisis

The political crisis came to a head in the mid-1970s, but had been developing as a strand of backlash politics, when busing was seen as a tool for forced integration. Several court cases led up to physical confrontation. *Green v. County School Bd. of New Kent Co.* (1968) approved court-ordered assignment of students to end segregation. *Swann v. Charlotte-Mecklenberg* (1971) ruled that preservation of neighborhood schools should not outweigh efforts to correct racial segregation and endorsed busing. *Keyes v. Denver School District #1* (1973) also endorsed busing outside of South to end de facto racial segregation. Yet, *Milliken v. Bradley* (1974) was a landmark 5-4 decision that insulated the suburbs from city/suburb busing proposals. The *Bradley* decision provided fearful whites the political ammunition necessary for resistance. Several characteristics of Boston public schools in 1974 included:

- 25% of students were black
- Only 0.5% of teachers were black
- No black principals
- Twelve of city's schools over 90% black
- Eleven of twelve schools at least fifty years old
- Newest predominantly black school twenty-six years old

Such disparities illustrated how two decades after the Supreme Court *Brown* decision in the Upper Northeast how racial tensions throughout the country were still alive and well.

## 313) Tax cutting

In the never-ending race for resources, stagflation experienced in the late 1970s contributed to budget deficits, triggering some tax increases. Inflation led to "bracket creep," pushing people into higher tax brackets when their real income has not increased. As incomes stagnated, taxes felt more burdensome even if they have not increased. Deregulation and cutbacks of government programs were seen as prime targets to help alleviate this tax burden upon individuals and larger governmental institutions. As a result, casualties included the Housing and Urban Development (HUD) budget cut by 30%. Comprehensive Employment and

Training Act (CETA) was eliminated. AFDC and food stamps were also cut by 14%.

The Economic Recovery Tax Act (1981) cut taxes 25% over three years and included cuts in capital gains, gift, and inheritance taxes. Such moves came on the heels of Proposition 13 (1978), or the People's Initiative to Limit Property Taxation as conservative principles eschewed personal responsibility and emphasized moving away from collective federal responsibility to shoulder the financial burden associated with the less fortunate. Social policy was now the problem rather than the solution.

314) **Len Bias**

A famously gifted University of Maryland basketball player who became the face of the oncoming crack cocaine epidemic that exploded upon the national scene in the early 1980s. Bias overdosed on crack cocaine and became a buzzword for all things dangerous associated with the drug. The continued emphasis on law and order allowed for more investment into law enforcement and drug task forces designed to eradicate and prevent future such incidents.

315) **Gordon Gekko**

A fictional movie character from a hit blockbuster movie from the 1980s entitled *Wall Street*, starring Charlie Sheen and Michael Douglas. Gekko, while symptomatic of avaricious corporate workers with no concept or consciousness of care for others, gave an oft-quoted speech to shareholders where he emphasized that "Greed is good!" This unofficial mantra was ironically used to justify one of the largest gaps between the haves and have-nots that the country has ever seen.

## CRITICAL QUESTS

316) **Objective:** *To understand the black image in the white mind*

Speaking of "black image in the white mind," consider this recent article about comments made by Reagan at that time, and how they still resonate (*<http://www.cnn.com/2012/01/23/politics/weflare-queen/>*). How much does the Negrophobic image depart from popularized images of black laziness in the aftermath of failed Reconstruction (i.e., "I pay for all!")?

**317) Objective:** *To understand the popularity of Gekko*
Look up "Greed is good!" and see how much of an imprint fictional Gordon Gekko has had upon the real business world. Specifically, look in *Fortune* magazine to see how many times Gekko has graced the cover.

© Fabio Freitas e Silva/Shutterstock.com

**318) Objective:** *To find the beneficiaries of affirmative action*
Look in *Time* magazine (<*http://ideas.time.com/2013/06/17/affirmative-action-has-helped-white-women-more-than-anyone/*>) and determine the following: What do you think of the idea that white women are the primary beneficiaries of affirmative action? Why is it then that blacks are most readily associated with affirmative action?

## CRITICAL QUESTIONS

**319) First consider:** "Prosperity Ministries" was a concept pioneered by conservative Christian California Orange County mega-preacher Robert Schuler that the good Lord would want for his righteous disciples to be blessed accordingly. How might such an approach fuel "righteous indignation" for the poor?

**320) Then contemplate:** How does Reaganomics account for budget deficit growth in the name of small government?

C. The "War on Drugs" based upon its execution, could be appropriately retitled, "War on (black) Thugs."

## CRITICAL CONCEPTS

321) **"War on Drugs"**

Initially launched during the 1970s, this initiative gained steam in the 1980s and was seen as a continuation of the law and order campaign where unsafe inner-city, urban areas all became euphemisms for black people who needed to be "put in their place" so that America's streets could feel safe again.

322) **100-to-1 Sentencing Ratio**

Mandatory minimums imposed by Federal Sentencing Guidelines stipulated that 100 grams of powdered cocaine was punishable for the same amount of jail time required by an individual who only had 1 gram of powder cocaine. Most crack cocaine offenders were nonwhite while most powder cocaine users were white.

323) **Crack vs. Powder**

Despite numerous studies in existence and circulation, no consensus to date has been achieved definitively determining that one substance is more potent than the other. In other words, the perception that crack cocaine (used by blacks) was more dangerous was a major factor in the tougher sentencing penalties.

324) **Hip Hop**

The latest strand of black innovation in music and culture, Rap Music and Hip Hop first came onto the scene in the late 1970s but truly began to penetrate mainstream circles in the mid-1980s as popularized by Hollywood mainstream movies *Beat Street* and *Breakin'*. This new art form of expression and style would become a mainstay over the next four decades at least, having transformed the way people express themselves forever.

325) **Distribution**

The 1980s saw the most unequal distribution of the fruits of economic growth since the 1920s' greed is good! Similar to economic patterns exhibited earlier by Robber Barons of old, a small number of Americans controlled access to most of the wealth.

# CRITICAL QUESTS

326) **Objective:** *To research the black image in the white mind*
In looking at how Negrophobia has changed over time, consider that during this time period, the War on Drugs began. Consider what various online sources have to say on the topic and see where you stand (*<http://en.wikipedia.org/wiki/Race_and_the_War_on_Drugs>*). While we may want to believe that the law is enforced equally, consider whether this is the case, especially in neighborhoods with a critical mass of minorities. See what the Drug Policy Alliance has to say and whether you agree or disagree (*<http://www.drugpolicy.org/race-and-drug-war>*). One thing is for sure, if the police want to find drugs today, all they have to do is go door to door in Beverly Hills...if they can make it past the security gate... (*<https://harpers.org/archive/2016/04/legalize-it-all/>*).

327) **Objective:** *To find out how the 100-to-1 ratio came to be*
Look up "Planet Rock: The Story of Hip Hop and the Crack Generation" (*<https://www.youtube.com/watch?v=zswrGZP7jUY>*) and see whether you agree that the ratio is justified.

328) **Objective:** *To appreciate the controversy of 100-to-1*
According to the data, is it conclusive whether crack cocaine smoked is more potent than powdered cocaine inhaled?

# CRITICAL QUESTIONS

329) **First consider:** The sentencing ratio has changed from 100-to-1 to 18-to-1. Does this solve the problem of mandatory sentencing guidelines?

330) **Then contemplate:** Why would Hip Hop group Run DMC make essentially a black protest song, entitled "Proud to Be Black," in the 1980s, some two decades after the civil rights movement crested with the Civil Rights Act?

# CRITICAL ANALYSIS OF BLACK PROGRESS

*"After Reagan, Presidents Clinton, Bush & Obama continued to shape an open America full of opportunity for all; many African Americans have benefited as a result but yet, so many still remain mired in the struggle."*

## PRIMARY IDEAS TO BEAR IN MIND:

A.  Ironically, while originally designed with blacks in mind, the passage of time has allowed data to show white women and others have statistically benefitted more from the 1964 Civil Rights Act.

B.  Kanye, Oprah, Will Smith, and LeBron James are examples of black success that still tread upon the tensions of romantic racialism seeing how they, like most famous blacks, are overwhelmingly sports figures/entertainers.

C.  President Obama's election for some ushered in a new "post-racial" society that signaled the elimination of racism of old; yet proof that elimination is difficult to muster.

A. Ironically, while originally designed with blacks in mind, the passage of time has allowed data to show white women and others have statistically benefitted more from the 1964 Civil Rights Act.

## CRITICAL CONCEPTS

**331) Affirmative Action**

A still controversial concept of aiding individuals with access to resources historically denied in the past as a means to "connect remedies to very particular public harms." Whereas theoretically many can "agree" on color-blind standards of nondiscrimination in addition to efforts at outreach and recruitment aimed at increasing applicants for scarce positions, in practice, disagreements rage where minorities appear to be chosen in light of ordinary grades and test scores—in other words, we can understand the acceptance of an exceptionally smart black, but an average one needs to justify his or her presence. Scholars such as Columbia University's Ira Katznelson argues that so many average whites have benefitted from white privilege or affirmative action themselves, that they only see it as problematic when another average black appears to get help and more access to resources which whites have been conditioned and entitled to expect.

For instance, southern congressional leaders made certain that the G.I. educational programs were directed not by Washington but by local white officials, businessmen, bankers, and college administrators who would honor past practices. Thousands of black veterans in the South—and the North as well—were denied housing and business loans, as well as admission to whites-only colleges and universities. Blacks were also excluded from job-training programs for careers in promising new fields like radio and electrical work, commercial photography, and mechanics. Instead, most blacks were channeled toward traditional, low-paying "black jobs" and small black colleges, pitifully underfinanced and ill equipped to meet the needs of a surging enrollment of returning soldiers. By October 1946, 6,500 former soldiers had been placed in nonfarm jobs by the employment service in Mississippi; 86% of the skilled and semiskilled jobs were filled by whites, 92% of the unskilled ones by blacks. In New York and northern New Jersey, "fewer than 100 of the 67,000 mortgages insured by the G.I. Bill supported home purchases by nonwhites." Discrimination continued as well in elite northern colleges. The University of Pennsylvania, along with Columbia (the least discriminatory of the Ivy League colleges), enrolled only 46 black students in its student body of 9,000 in 1946. Black colleges did not have places for 70,000 black veterans in 1947. At the same time, white universities doubled their enrollments and prospered with the infusion of public and private funds, students with their G.I. benefits.

332) **Civil Rights Act 1991**

Even though signed under conservative President Bush, is indicative of how the continued struggle for dignity and respect for blacks was far from over. The 1964 landmark Civil Rights Act apparently was not the cure-all that many were looking for.

333) **First "black" president**

Affectionate nickname given to Democratic Arkansas President William Jefferson Clinton. Clinton in the 1990s was the "closest thing" to a non-white president the political climate had seen before, given his more liberal views and willingness to go on national television with a black host (i.e., Arsenio Hall) and play jazz instrumental tunes on a tenor saxophone.

334) **Federal Emergency Management Assistance**

FEMA became a household name in the wake of the Category 5 Katrina hurricane that devastated the New Orleans area with flooding in 2005. International criticism poured in over the tardy response time to a mostly black populace in contrast with other federal emergencies.

335) **Clarence Thomas**

Supreme Court nominee to replace the late Thurgood Marshall in 1991. National narratives about unchecked black sexuality were on display when Anita Hill came forward accusing Thomas of sexual harassment while the two worked together at the Equal Employment Opportunity Commission. Thomas, a conservative appointee, was the second African American to ever serve on the Supreme Court.

## CRITICAL QUESTS

336) **Objective:** *To understand the black image in the white mind*

Consider the national discussions raging about sexual harassment as seen through the lens of "bad black behavior" with the Thomas/Hill interplay. How many other instances have blacks been used as the definitive standard with which to judge status quo behavior? What about Michael Vick and dog fighting? Tiger Woods and infidelity? Ray Rice and domestic violence? Adrian Peterson and corporal punishment? Richard Sherman and interview etiquette?

337) **Objective:** *To understand the white image in the black mind*

Is this "Jurassic World" clip mere innocent entertainment [*<https://www.youtube.com/watch?v=DCRiyYagtig>*]? Or, the coincidental fact that the white male is the alpha male (and for those of you who saw the movie, successfully manipulates the velociraptors later within the movie to attack one of their "own kind" with him leading the way on a motor-cycle...)? This is similar to the white alpha male status of Superman, Iron Man, Batman, James Bond, and so forth.

Finally, as for image, when we consider the "high heels" scene of *Jurassic World*, the question for us to consider is how does this glamorized imagery affect us? This is tricky due to the unique dynamic white women experience colloquially referred to as "Home Court/Field Advantage," whereby while suppressed and subjugated relative to white men, white women nonetheless enjoy a privileged position in relation to virtually all other racial/gender demographics by virtue of their special "in-house" relationship with white men as the mothers, daughters, wives, etc., of white men. Thus, while we may not think of it this way, white women are frequently the direct beneficiaries and targets of white male prowess and consequently are uniquely positioned to leverage their privileged status for equality with other white men.

Thus, it is not surprising that whenever we see a "first" with respect to women within public social circles, it frequently "just happens" to be a white woman. We must be careful, for within these contexts, "women" actually becomes a coded euphemism for "white women," for that is who practically has such access to such power and who the power structure has a vested interest in placating. White men in power, even if only acting out of their own self-interest, realize that it is not feasibly sustainable for them to be dominant and exclusive in all professional affairs, when white women are included within their personal affairs in so many ways. The question then becomes when it comes to the structuring, systematizing, and sharing of resources, what incentive exists for white males in power to make such accommodations for those outside of their inner circle—especially among race and gender lines?

Additionally consider the following news of "social progress for women" as just described within a traditionally male dominated enclave such as sports:

*Introduction to African–American Studies*

- *<http://sports.yahoo.com/news/nfl-hires-sarah-thomas-1st-female-official-142522519--nfl.html>*
- *<http://sports.yahoo.com/blogs/mlb-big-league-stew/a-s-hire-justine-siegal--making-her-the-first-female-coach-for-an-mlb-team-222835376.html>*
- *<https://www.yahoo.com/style/jen-welter-becomes-first-female-nfl-coach-125255812243.html>*

338) **Objective:** *To understand continuity over time*

Look up "segregated schools" today and take note of what results you receive. How can data support the existence of segregated schools today despite the social progress made thus far more than half a century after the original *Brown* decision?

## CRITICAL QUESTIONS

339) **First consider:** Given all that what blacks continue to experience in this country with respect to "the struggle," what exactly did the civil rights movement accomplish?

© Julie Clopper/Shutterstock.com

340) **Then contemplate:** Look up the accompanying link and decide, how much of the present is tied to the past? [*<http://news.yahoo.com/har-vard-unc-sued-over-admission-policies-183827793.html>*]

B. Kanye, Oprah, Will Smith, and LeBron James are examples of black success that still tread upon the tensions of romantic racialism seeing how they, like most famous blacks, are overwhelmingly sports figures/entertainers.

## CRITICAL CONCEPTS

341) *Cosby Show*

An example of mainstream, wholesome entertainment. The show depicted blacks as professional, financially successful and functional. The show was an unqualified mainstream success and was a fixture in mainstream culture. The *Cosby Show*'s legacy is now in dispute in the wake of several allegations brought forth from several individuals, some with claims dating back to the 1970s.

342) **Carol Mosley Braun**

First black female national senator elected into office from Illinois. Less than ten blacks have served as national senators in the whole history of the United States of America.

343) **Tiana**

The name of the first black Disney princess who debuted in the animated movie, *The Princess and the Frog*. Tiana however, was a frog for most of the movie.

344) **Black Entertainment Television**

BET was an attempt to provide alternate programming in contrast to traditional mainstream choices. The channel was criticized for lack of original programming and was eventually bought out by white owners at Viacom.

345) **FUBU**

An acronym that stands for "For Us, By Us." An alternate clothing option provided in contrast to traditional clothing lines that did not prominently feature blacks. It represented an entrepreneurial impulse to highlight black existence in the marketplace. FUBU was eventually bought out.

## CRITICAL QUESTS

346) **Objective:** *To understand what the current image of blacks is in the white mind*

Are things better? After all, we see Kanye, Oprah, Obama all as examples of black success. But are these the exceptions or the norm? How many

*Introduction to African-American Studies*

blacks still suffer today from discrimination? Not to be funny, but do you know any blacks personally? If so, how well do you know them? Have you spent considerable time in their homes? Have you ever discussed their experiences? Or are you reluctant? Do you not want to say the wrong thing? Or do you assume that they appear to be happy?

347) *Objective: To understand continued white resistance*
Look up the following article and determine whether this group is part of the fringe or "silent majority": <*http://www.azfamily.com/news/White-Man-March-planned-for-Tempe-Saturday-250377641.html*>

348) *Objective: To find out what the black mass is doing:* <*http://www.the-root.com/articles/culture/2014/11/mental_health_care_still_lacking_for_those_in_poverty.html*>. After reading this article link, how do you think the legacy of poverty has affected African American existence?

## CRITICAL QUESTIONS

349) **First consider:** Who is Famous Amos? Where is he now?

350) **Then contemplate:** What economic incursions from African Americans have been wholly independent and self-sustaining?

## B. President Obama's election for some ushered in a new "post-racial" society that signaled the elimination of racism of old; yet proof that elimination is difficult to muster.

## CRITICAL CONCEPTS

351) **Barack Obama**
The forty-fourth U.S. president and arguably the "first black president." Obama has been at the center of an involved conversation about race and identity. His personal story is different from the "typical" narrative since he was raised by his white mother in Indonesia and Ha-

© Yury Shchipakin/Shutterstock.com

wai'i. It is also unclear how much of a factor is Obama's fair complexion and how it plays into romantic facialist notions of nonthreatening black males who can be trusted.

352) **"You lie!"**

U.S. Representative Joe Wilson shouted this phrase from the galley inside the Capitol building during President Obama's first State of the Union address. Wilson postured in the following days about whether to provide an apology and was actually able to raise $2 million on the campaign trail.

353) **Beergate**

African American Harvard University professor Skip Gates was arrested for disorderly conduct on his own residential property. Early in Obama's term, he and Vice-President Joe Biden hosted a beer session between Gates and the arresting officer as a way to broker the peace. Obama was criticized by police unions for being overly critical and was criticized by liberals for not being critical enough.

354) **Donald Trump**

A businessman who felt his brash and blunt style is what the country needs, is the latest iteration of white males who use fear-mongering as a tactic to "take back the country." Trump, akin to Nixon's silent majority and southern strategy, has made incendiary comments of a racist and xenophobic nature without much criticism or fanfare since he merely represents what so many privately agree with.

355) **Racism 2.0**

The concept that racism of old was overt, obvious, and offensive. New racism is subtle, suave, and sophisticated. Thus, many racially historical patterns are repeated, but are simply made more palatable because they appear less offensive in nature.

## CRITICAL QUESTS

356) **Objective:** *To research the black image in the white mind*

Look up the latest mainstream movie release STARRING a black character as the central protagonist. Do you have difficulty? If so, why? If the civil rights era was successful, why would we not see more visual proof of this cultural acceptance of blacks as individuals worthy of our time and imagination as represented through movie heroes? Why then the continued "segregation of the mind" in Hollywood? What does the paucity of primary black representation tell us?

357) **Objective:** *To find whether there is "race" in the presidency*
Consider these episodes involving Obama. Are they general to any president or are they specifically racially flavored?
- Senator Harry Reid compliments Obama as "articulate"
- *Boston Globe* – watermelon reference in political cartoon
- *New Yorker* – fist bump and terrorist imagery
- *NY Post* – Obama analogized to an ape in a political cartoon
- Watermelon White House email
    o Dean Grose, mayor of the small southern California town of Los Alamitos, thought it was funny. It was an email of a watermelon patch superimposed on the lawn of the White House. In an incredible lapse of judgment, he forwarded the email to members of the community with a heading that read, "No Easter Egg hunt this year." His alarm bells should have been going off. But Grose just dug himself in deeper: "The way things are today, you gotta laugh every now and then. I wanna see the coloring contests."

358) **Objective:** *To appreciate the continued "struggle"*
Consider these national cases that all happened after Obama was elected in November 2008:
- Oscar Grant
- Trayvon Martin
- Michael Brown
- Freddie Gray

Consider what these deaths of unarmed black males say about the value of black life dating back to Emmett Till.

## CRITICAL QUESTIONS

359) **First consider:** When considering the contemporary movement as symbolized by #blacklivesmatter, what does it say about structural and institutional racism if one of the more critical movements for black rights occurred while a "black man" was president?

360) **Then contemplate:** Has Obama's election symbolized the end or evolution of racism?

# conclusion

In conclusion, our time will be brief.

Upon reflection, in taking a "well-rounded" introduction or 360-degree angle of understanding for African American history, we observed that the story begins with the early arrival of Africans to America; it was a sad beginning to this evolving story. One that became esteeped in enslavement and race. This controversial contradiction of enslavement within a "land of freedom" helped push the nation towards its first and only Civil War, a pivotal period whereby physical freedom for all was secured; yet tensions leading up to USA's costliest war not fully resolved upon war's conclusion.

Afterwards, the nation attempted systemic healing through what is now known as Black Reconstruction, or rather the country's first, earnest attempt to practice equality post-enslavement; revolutionary, controversial and short-lived. This revolutionary period was short-lived for American society observed physical freedom in theory, but in practice such freedom was compromised by segregationist social policies informally and colloquially organized known as Jim Crow's Reign.

Yet, despite existing social challenges, the worst in American society brought out some of the best in African American society as evidenced with the blossoming of high artistic, intellectual and spiritual expression during the Black Renaissance. Such new glimpses of humanity for African Americans helped spawn the Great Migration, a key period that helps explain current demographic living patterns, particularly in large, metropolitan urban areas; many African Americans left the south for the 'big city' in search of the American Dream.

Yet, such dreams were difficult to consistently make reality as the nation entered the period of WWII and Beyond, an ironic period whereby even when fighting fascism abroad, African Americans had to still fight racism domestically (even within the "colorblind" armed services). Such continued frustration led directly to the rise of the black freedom movement, where African Americans took a significant step in raising awareness about their quest for humanity, dignity and respect. Soon after, the initial quest by African Americans was broadened into an initiative that secured more protections for all Americans, including African Americans with the well-known civil rights movement of which many Americans are now aware.

While the civil rights era is hailed as a breakthrough period for race relations, nonetheless, the sour distaste of war also soured the outlook of many African Americans still longsuffering for equality; more pointed critiques emerged as a result courtesy of the two polarizing movements of Vietnam and black radicalism. But skepticism was not isolated to African Americans.

After decades of federal social programming, the government was now seen as the problem; Reagan's "small government" and "War on Drugs" policies significantly impacted African Americans accordingly during the peak of twentieth-century conservative politics affectionately known as Reaganomics. Yet, after Reagan, Presidents Clinton, Bush, and Obama continued to shape an open America full of opportunity for all; many African Americans have benefited as a result but yet, so many still remain mired in the struggle.

Which is why critical analysis of black progress is still required.

In essence, before parting ways, the reader must observe the argument that African American history is in fact American history—it is quite difficult to tell the story of the one without invoking the other. To this end, now that we have reached the end, it is now appropriate to redirect our attention to the very beginning. As in the *cover of this manuscript*. If one studies the cover illustration with a careful eye, they will notice that the American flag is central to the picture, but yet and still, the flag is slightly off center. Perhaps this symbolizes that the philosophies and ideals undergirding America are spot on target, but yet in practice, it appears the great United States of America has been plagued by inconsistencies in placing the theory into practice, especially as applied en masse to African Americans over time.

Additionally, the flag is upheld by what appears to be a hand "of color"—reflect upon this ambiguity as African American history is for everyone, not just African Americans. Thus, it COULD be the hand of an African American, or it could be a white American whose hand is ironically made darker by the American flag's shadow. This photo is quite delicious indeed for part of the flag is clearly in focus while part of the flag is blurry—much like the current picture on race relations concerning African Americans.

Lastly, the thatch pattern in the background of the cover (and also as seen in circles surrounding the page numbers in the text) subtly conveys the message of two worlds connecting, one "African" and one "American." For when it comes to race relations in general and specifically for African Americans, it appears that data and experience indicate that often we inhabit the same planet, yet different worlds.

Where we go from here is for you to decide. Now you have been properly "introduced," be sure to continue looking at the issues from all degrees and all angles.

For once new information is acquired, new insights are often inspired.

Once new data is digested, new decisions are often determined.

Once new concepts are understood, new conclusions are created.

May you remain "A Critical Reader…"

CPSIA information can be obtained
at www.ICGtesting.com
Printed in the USA
LVOW02s1409210616

493435LV00002B/3/P